χ

Five Four Whiskey

ROBERT SWEATMON

FIVE FOUR WHISKEY

A MEMORY OF WAR

WESTHOLME
Yardley

Westholme Publishing, LLC
904 Edgewood Road
Yardley, Pennsylvania 19067
Visit our Web site at www.westholmepublishing.com

First Printing October 2014
10 9 8 7 6 5 4 3 2 1
ISBN: 978-1-59416-207-7
Also available as an eBook.

Printed in the United States of America.

*To the members of the 2nd Platoon, C Company,
1st Battalion of the 5th Mechanized Infantry,
who became home and family in a time that,
despite this writing, defies description.*

"Five Four Whiskey, . . . Five Four Whiskey, . . . Niner Four Oscar."

It was a simple radio recognition code from the past.

"Five Four Whiskey, this is Niner Four Oscar."

The words were nonsensical to anyone who had not played an active role in the nightmare. It was not a threatening message. On the contrary, it was a sound that had meant help was within our grasp. It had come over static-filled airways many times, to reassure us that we were not alone. It was the thread of life and the promise of returning home to us all, yet as it sounded out of the twilight of my dreams, it brought terrors and remembrance of a time that we are just now coming to understand.

"Five Four Whiskey, this is Niner Four Oscar. If you are unable to respond, break squelch twice."

As always, I would awake from the dream, and the faceless, metallic voice from the past would lose its hold on me. I would rise, shower, dress, and drive headlong into the workaday world, which is the center of the reality we live in. Days and months would turn into years, and the prospect that the dream was only just that seemed more and more the consideration of a sane man. It was, after all, long past and half a world away.

Nineteen sixty-nine was a year among years. The music of the time described it better than mere prose could ever attempt to do. The radios of America wailed along the AM frequencies, inciting the young to heed the beat of a different drummer. They cried out to us in louder and louder decibels, and we listened. We swore to wear flowers in our hair if we ever went to San Francisco, while our parents swayed gently to the voice of a more rational Tony Bennett, who only claimed to have left his heart in the Bay City. The rest of us seemed to have left our sanity there.

It was a time in which the youth of America had finally kicked open the door to the future and seemed to be standing, wistfully scratching their heads, while trying to decide which way to go. Simon and Garfunkel serenaded us into wishing that we were nonfeeling rocks, while Bob Dylan demanded that we admit to the changing times. The greats of music and drama followed the chemically induced logic of Timothy Leary and tuned in, turned on, and dropped out. We were all taken aback by the sudden and unfettered freedom of the drug culture. It offered us an alternative to all forms of discipline. It was, in fact, the wholesale flight of America from its mundane daily duties that became the real siren's call. It was the absolution from having to take out the trash that caught us all unaware, and myself in particular unprepared. Nineteen sixty-nine caught me with my pants down. In my case, California dreamin' was becoming a reality.

In 1969, I was at the top and bottom of my form as a young man from a good family. I suppose this statement needs a little explanation. My parents certainly thought that it needed some explanation. I had managed the ultimate catastrophe of the '60s. I was a twenty-year-old college student who was no longer in college. This is no big thing today, nor would it have been in most periods of our history. In 1969, it could mean only one thing for a boy who came from working stock and was no longer protected from the draft by the infamous 2-S deferment. It meant that it was only a matter of time until that young man was wearing the uniform of his country and showing the flag in other parts of the world, the most prominent of those parts being the now-defunct Republic of South Vietnam. Somehow, I don't believe that this is what those radio personalities had in mind when they shoveled all that Dylan manure at us. I wonder how many of them ended up crawling around in Southeast Asia, trying not to get a third eye? I don't remember seeing Wolf Man Jack at Dau Tieng or Peter, Paul, and Mary in the Ho Bo Woods. Talk about being five hundred miles from my home. They didn't have a clue.

What I'm trying to say is that the songs and movies and stars of the day literally sold us down the river. They painted pictures of life without pain or standards or responsibility. They went to corporate meetings, met contract restrictions, and paid their taxes while portraying to the masses that they were devoid of such dull and tiring chores. They painted the picture so well that we bought it. We didn't just buy it to hang over the couch. We bought it to move into. It is said that neurotics build castles in the sky, and psychotics move in. Well, I moved in, along with much of the youth of America. I moved in and began paying the bills for such a move. I'm still paying them today. We all are.

At this point, I'm sure there is a well-established alarm going off somewhere in your subconscious. It would be warning you of the man on the street corner who is dressed in faded combat fatigues and a bush hat, four decades after the fact. The man now has gray hair and a paunch but seems stuck somewhere in that 365 days he spent on the other side of the world a lifetime ago. The warning bell has probably trained you to smile pleasantly and step around him, unless you find it impossible to courteously avoid a confrontation, which you usually bring to a close with a dollar bill or two. I know this discomfort. I experience it myself. I go through it along with you and hundreds of thousands of veterans of the Vietnam conflict who did not fall into the abyss upon returning home. I step around those poor, experience-locked victims, fumble for cash, and then walk on. I walk on like all the rest who heard the songs, took the fall, and returned to pick up the pieces that were shattered when we were swallowed whole by the military and the times. I walk on, but when I think I am safely out of range, I look back. I look back and strain to see through the gauzelike curtain of the years. I look to see if it is a face I might have known, a name I might remember. I look and I find myself angry and then horrified. How much of a step would it have been for me to go from hearing static-tattered voices in my dreams to standing there on the street like the Ghost of Christmas Past. I wonder what made the difference?

Track One

CUE: *Bad Moon Rising*, CREEDENCE CLEARWATER REVIVAL

Whump!

The sound pulled me from an uneasy sleep. I rolled over to look at Lester, but he was only a dim shadow in the dark.

"What's going on?"

My question was no more than a hoarse whisper, but Lester placed his hand on my arm in such a way that I knew to be quiet. It was a part of the language of the night.

Whump!

This time I not only heard the sound but felt it. It was the sound of our defensive Claymore mines going off. I rolled over to reach for my weapon, and scampering feet suddenly burst out of the darkness, jumped the rice dike, came down on my left leg, and disappeared into the night. I sat up and snapped off two shots into the darkness and lay back down. I knew immediately that it had been the wrong thing to do. It could have given away our position.

We lay silently in the dark, that dark-of-the-moon kind of dark. Lester and I held one end of the line while MacAvoy and Clements held the other. In between were French, Gilreath, Oscar Solis, and Lieutenant Clark. Doc Glover was probably the medic that night, and it's possible that "Lurch" or Joe Raber may have been there as well. I simply can't remember. The years have been too many, and try as I might, I cannot peer down that line in the dark and see anybody else.

Something moved beyond the rice dike, and Lester began to set off his Claymores. I dug for my clackers, or triggers, and set off the mine that was placed out in front of our position, but I waited to fire the mine that was set behind us. I didn't know what might be out there. The silence set in again. As I looked to my right, I could make out Lester's shadow. He was bending low over the dike, sighting against the skyline. It was a way of maximizing the light on dark-of-the-moon nights. Down the line I could hear the voice of Lieutenant Clark calling for artillery illumination. If we could get light from the sky we could see who they were, where they were.

Wham!

This sound was different. It was a flat, loud blast that filled our lungs with acrid smoke and the air about us with a thicker darkness than before. No one knew where it had come from, but each of us knew that it had been a hand grenade. We began to throw our own grenades out into the darkness and pray for the artillery to light the skies.

"Hit it."

It was Gilreath's voice and it was almost devoid of emotion, but we all knew what it meant. I tried to make myself as small as I possibly could and I waited. It seemed like an eternity until the blast came. When it did, people got hurt.

Wham!

The soft, muddy dirt flew all over us. We pulled back up tight against the rice dike to see who was hurt and determine where it had come from.

French was bent over holding his face. When Lester got over to look at him, he found that a piece of the grenade was completely through the bridge of his nose. Nothing else was touched. Lieutenant Clark had not been so lucky. He had been closest to the blast.

Clark's hand and his weapon had deflected much of the force of the blast, but he had taken shrapnel to the face and was bleeding profusely from his left eye. Oscar Solis had been hit in the foot while crawling away from the grenade, but he would not let us know that until much later. Lester had caught a piece of fragment in his knee, but like Oscar let no one know he was hit. The worst of it was the revelation from Gilreath that the grenade had come from a hand that had simply reached over the dike. As the artillery began illuminating the skies above us, we faced the realization that we were lying on one side of a twelve-inch berm of earth and that the local guerrillas, the Viet Cong, or VC, were on the other.

Lieutenant Clark was in considerable pain, but his voice was calm. He was still in command. He gave orders to call for gunship support and a medevac dustoff, or helicopter evacuation of our wounded, and then his voice carried down the line.

"Lester, look over that dike and see how many are over there."

At that moment, Lester Lorig won my undying admiration. Without a moment's hesitation, he sat upright, looked over that berm, counted heads, and lay back down. He announced that there were nine people on the other side of that thin mound of earth, and my heart went into arrest. At that moment, we were so close to the enemy that we could have fought the war with a tire tool.

Lieutenant Clark passed the word that we would have to pull back to a position a hundred yards or so to our rear. Since Lester and I were on one end of the line and MacAvoy was on the other, we would cover the withdrawal. As we poised ourselves for the move, it struck me that we had heard nothing from the people on the other side of the dike. I will always wonder what they were doing. Maybe they were trying to pull out as well. It doesn't really matter, because all at once Lester and I began pouring fire over the dike while the others picked up the lieutenant and French and disappeared into the fading edges of the artillery-born light. The scene in front of us looked amazingly like it was part of an old silent movie. The strange pulsating light from the artillery flares and the highlights made by muzzle flashes caused the twitching bodies on the ground to appear almost ghostlike. Then it went dark again.

The artillery flares had gone out, leaving Lester and me standing blind in the middle of the rice field. We dropped and hugged the ground and tried to catch our breath when it dawned on us that we had set no sign or signal to identify ourselves to the rest of our ambush patrol, which waited out there in the dark. Ambush patrols were sent out to kill the enemy and harass its movements under cover of darkness. At that moment, Lester and I had no desire to become victims of such tactics from our own guys, but there was no real way to tell them it was us moving toward them in the gloom. We finally started running toward their position, screaming at the top of our lungs that it was us. It must have worked. No one threw a shot in our direction, and just as we jumped over another rice dike to join the others, the sky lit up again. God bless the artillery.

When we got back it was evident that the lieutenant was getting worse. His voice was strained now, but he was still very much in control. He had contacted the dustoff chopper, which was inbound to our location, but it was our location that was a problem. It was pitch black when the flares weren't up, and there were still bad guys out there, somewhere. We needed to show the chopper exactly which part of the Vietnamese dark we were in.

This feat of magic was usually pulled off with the use of a small, flashing strobe light, which helps locate friendly soldiers from the air without telling the rest of the world about it. Lieutenant Clark always carried a strobe light, but unfortunately it was back at the ambush site with gear that had been left behind.

"We have to have that strobe." Lieutenant Clark's voice was calm and steady in spite of his pain. "We can't land the chopper without it."

Lester got up, picked up his weapon, and crawled over the dike and into the darkness. His voice trailed behind him.

"Are you coming, Stoney?"

I heard another voice break the uneasy silence.

"Coming, Mother."

I couldn't believe it. It was me who had said that. I had never been so astounded in my life. There I was, still in one piece after all but rubbing shoulders with the VC, and now I was following Lester Lorig back to the same spot to look for an overrated flashlight.

By the time we reached the ambush site, the darkness seemed even thicker than before. We began going through the equipment left on the side of the dike by feel alone. Suddenly, Lester grabbed my arm and held up something in the dark that must have been the bag. He made motions to me that we should go back when we were both frozen in place by a sound. It was a low moan. It came again and we sat down, silently. There was silence for a moment, and then the moaning started again, but this time it was answered by another voice, speaking in Vietnamese. Lester handed me the bag and then fished out a hand grenade. When we were both poised for flight, Lester rolled the grenade over the dike, and we ran like hell for a count of three and then fell on our faces in the dirt.

Wham!

The blast kicked up dirt and smoke and covered us with both. We picked up and ran back to the platoon's location, only to discover that we had brought back the wrong bag. It was filled with carbine magazines. We would have to go back. If we couldn't call the bird in, our wounded would have to wait until morning. Even a coward like me could not stand the thought of that, so back we went into the night.

When we reached the dike, it took almost no time at all to locate the bag and the strobe, but before we could start back, the moaning began again. It was the kind of sound that crawls up your spine and into your soul. It was awful, and it was my turn to toss the frag. I untwisted the safety wire and pulled out the retaining pin. On a silent count of three, I lobbed the grenade over the dike and hit Lester on the back as a sign to go. We ran and dropped as before. This time we were covered with more than dirt. Something fell on my back. It hit with a flat thud and just lay there. I still don't know what it was, but my imagination conjured up gruesome pictures.

Back at the platoon, we discovered that this time we had the strobe light, but it was no longer working. We had no light, and the dustoff chopper was circling our position. C. L. Clements handed me a white star cluster flare. He instructed me to fire it along the ground immediately away from our position. Clements was always amazingly bright. No wonder he was our platoon sergeant. I fired the flare along the ground until it came to rest, brightly burning about fifty yards from our position. Just like it was called from the sky, the helicopter made a short turn and sat down a few yards from the flare.

We carried French, Lieutenant Clark, and Oscar to the chopper. There were a few terse words that came clumsily, then we stepped back and watched the bird rise up into the night sky. The rotor wash pummeled us and then ebbed as the aircraft gained altitude. It hung there only a moment and then tipped forward, bit into the air, and was gone. We were left standing in the blackness to deal with what still lay out there in the dark.

The dustoff chopper was only gone a few minutes when the Cobra gunship arrived. It swung low over our heads and swept the line of trees in the distance with a spray of minigunfire that cut the night with a loud, sustained belch. The red trail of destruction lit the night with a hellish glow, which should have unnerved us all.

Instead, we felt protected and in control once again. The gunship hung over us until we were satisfied that the wood line was clear, then rose high and veered off. The sky fell dark again and we were alone.

The rest of the night we watched, waiting for something to come and get us and hoping it would not. Lester and I took our customary places at the end of the line and lay quietly, peering out into the darkness. We said nothing.

Track Two

CUE: *The Letter*, THE BOX TOPS

There are letters and there are letters. There are those that often make such changes in a young man's life that he always remembers them. He remembers the way the envelope felt in his hand when he took it from the mailbox and the sound it made as he ripped it open. These are often letters that announce that he has been accepted into the university of his choosing, or telling him that he has won a coveted scholarship. Sometimes the letter is penned in the delicate hand of his sweetheart, telling him that she will be his bride or even that she never wants to see him again. These epistles are often life changing and always kept in the memory as stark reminders of those moments. In my case, I don't think I saw the letter at all. In fact, I have no recollection as to ever having seen it, but it changed my life all the same.

Summer '69 was warm and promising. I was starting my second season working as a stuntman in the gunfight shows at the Six Flags Over Texas amusement park. It was one of those perfect jobs where I got to play cowboys for a living and no one called me silly or irresponsible for doing so. In fact, I was paid pretty well for falling off buildings and trains and the like. I was sitting in the sun one afternoon, cleaning my pistol and watching the crowds amble by, when a pretty young girl came out of the Crazy Horse Saloon to tell me that I had a phone call from my father. I was a bit panicked. My family never called me at the park. I was convinced that someone must be close to dying. As it turned out, that someone was me.

"I have a letter here for you."

My father's voice was flat and unusually devoid of humor. I thought maybe it was the sound of his voice in the phone that made him seem so strained. It was not.

"It's from the president of the United States."

My heart skipped a beat. In those days, every young man who was out of school and healthy stood a pretty good chance of getting his draft notice. I had already been called for a physical and had been simply ignoring the fact that the other shoe was about to drop. I listened to my father's voice read the letter to me over that beat-up phone in the back of the Crazy Horse Saloon. When he came to the last words, they burned themselves into my memory so that I can hear them even today.

"You have ten days to report."

I walked out into the crowded street and looked about me. The festive decorations of the amusement park seemed suddenly very dear to me. I listened to the speakers that played western movie music all day long to add atmosphere to the western sets, and I realized that I would not hear them again for a long time.

"You have ten days to report."

The words kept bouncing around in my head. How can they expect a man to wrap up his entire life in only ten days? In actuality, my life was so trivial that it only took a few hours to wrap it up. I can honestly say that I don't remember everything that happened during those fast ten days. I remember a party or two and one really bad hangover, and then I was riding on a plane bound for my part in history. It was a part I neither asked for nor shirked but experienced along with millions of others. I have often wondered what happened to that letter.

My family background was military in its very nature. My grandfather had run away from home and joined the US Cavalry at the tender age of sixteen. He chased Pancho Villa to Vera Cruz and went to France with Pershing in World War I. My father, who was my grandfather's only son, joined the Marine Corps to be a pilot in World War II and was a member of the storied VMA 121 attack squadron during the Korean conflict. Some of my earliest memories are of life on Marine bases and knowledge of the intense pride my family felt in military service.

By summer '69, my family was faced with a bit of a split in their sentiments about the conflict then raging in Southeast Asia. Their loyalty to the country and their pride in our armed forces was uncompromised, but their desire to see another son put in harm's way was shaking their resolve a bit. When I took my leave of my aging grandfather, he was stoic and unusually silent. When we hugged at parting, he began to shed tears. I had never seen that before. It troubled me, and I confess that I was taken aback by such forceful emotion coming from that old and usually very hard man. It would be decades before I understood that moment. My grandfather had shouldered arms and carried the flag through the last cavalry campaign in American history. He had traveled across the ocean to survive midnight raids, bayonet attacks, and poison gas in a great effort they called the war to end all wars. A generation later, he sent his only son, twice, into the same madness. Now he was watching a third generation put on the uniform and leave home following the same kind of promises. It would be long after his death that I came to realize that the tears he shed were not for me. They were for all of us.

Basic training has not changed all that much since the days of George Washington and the Continental Army. It is a simple and direct attack on the individuality of the human. The need to take any number of individuals, from any number of backgrounds, with any number of beliefs, and mold them into soldiers who have an undying love of country, an indisputable subservience to authority, and the physical stamina to march through hell and back, is a monumental task. When you throw in the fact that it must be done and done well in eight and one-half weeks, the task seems insurmountable. The odd fact is that the army has been doing exactly that since Baron von Steuben drilled the first American soldiers during the winter at Valley Forge. Basic-training stories are the staple of a serviceman's memoirs and are the subject of any number of Hollywood epics involving the military. They all center on the iron will of the drill instructor and can be summed up in a Caesar-like quote: "I came, I saw, he conquered." It is pretty much the same for everybody. The only thing I will mention here is my sad case of decision making that will lead me to the rest of this saga.

Upon arriving at Fort Bliss, Texas, the whole bunch of new recruits were subjected to a battery of written tests. After each test, the group would be herded outside for a smoke break, and then, in time, some names were called and a smaller number of future Sad Sacks would be marched back inside to take more tests. This continued until there was only a small group left. This reduced number was marched off to another building where they were given the officer's qualifying test. I was a part of this last group and was told that I had qualified for Officers Candidate School (OCS) if I did well enough in basic training. This sounded great and led me into a trap that I sort of laid for myself.

During basic training, those of us in the OCS group were occasionally called away from training and given psychological tests and interviewed and questioned ad infinitum about our loyalties and the state of our patriotism. When we graduated from basic training, we were called in and seated at a table. Impressive looking papers were placed in front of us, and we were instructed to sign them. Being curious by nature, I asked what the papers meant. The officer in charge smiled and told me that one was a discharge as a draftee and an enlisted man, and the other was a contract. The contract stated that I was volunteering to serve three years after the date of my commission as a second lieutenant in the infantry. I took all this in and then began to ask more questions. I asked how long it would take to get this commission. The answer was nine months or more. I asked if this meant that I would be sent to Vietnam as an infantry platoon leader. The answer was yes, at least once. I asked what would happen if I didn't sign. I was told that I would remain an enlisted man for two years in whatever assignment I was given.

I may not be the sharpest knife in the drawer, but it didn't take me too long to add things up and figure out that if I signed the contract, after the nine months it took to get my commission, I would have to serve three years, and I was going into combat as the head of a rifle platoon. If I didn't sign anything, I had only two years to serve in whatever job they might give me. Only 10 percent of the army is involved in combat. The other 90 percent stacks C rations and washes underwear and the like. The odds simply made my mind up for me. I refused to sign and was sent back to the ranks and assigned a military occupational status of 11B. In military jargon that's Eleven Bravo, and it refers to the light weapons infantry. I took a deep breath and was sent straight as an arrow to killer school at Fort Ord in California. From there the next stop would, in all likelihood, be the Republic of South Vietnam. I often wonder where I would have ended up if I had made the other choice. I certainly wouldn't have gotten shot at any more than I did with C Company, and at least someone would have called me "Sir."

Track Three

CUE: *A Hard Day's Night*, THE BEATLES

I stared out into the night, and the blackness stared back at me. Another midnight found me exhausted and aching from the day's exertions in a land that posted temperatures of 115 degrees as a daily occurrence. Our 2nd Platoon had drawn ambush patrol duty for the third night in a row, and the fatigue was beginning to show in everyone concerned. As I leaned back against the rice dike and tried to peer into the darkness behind us, I could see only the shadows of what I knew to be the tree line, which was some one hundred yards behind us. Nothing seemed to move out there in the darkness. Nothing but those strange, night wiggles in your vision, which fool us all into seeing things that are simply not there. I would be awake for two hours if I could take that, then I would wake Lester and he would watch for two hours. After that, we would switch off until dawn as best we could. Whoever was in the best shape would take the final watch, which is the most critical time. With the coming of the dawn also came the most dangerous hour. In the early light, men often do not see what is coming at them and can be more easily overcome.

By February 1970, C Company, 1st Battalion of the 5th Mechanized Infantry, was terribly shorthanded. December and January had taken their toll on the troop roster, and now the company was so undermanned that the same men were going out on ambush patrol night after night. Exhaustion was beginning to cause mistakes, and the mistakes were costing lives. Two nights before, an ambush patrol from the 3rd Platoon had all fallen asleep, allowing the VC to walk into their midst. When the enemy was discovered, close firing took American as well as enemy lives. Now, in the gloom, I sat rubbing my eyes and trying to stay awake long enough to give Lester a little time to sleep. He needed the rest, and I needed him to do the same for me.

The radio hissed and I took the handset and pressed it to my ear.

"Alpha Papa One, Alpha Papa One. This is Romeo Niner Five. I need a sit rep, over." The company would call us once every hour to ask for a situation report, using the cryptic radio language of the army.

I reached for the corner of the green blanket on which I was lying and covered my head with it. I pressed the button on the side of the handset and whispered a response over the static-filled airways.

"This is Alpha Papa One. I have negative sit rep at this time, over."

The sound of squelch hissed, and I pressed the handset hard against my ear to diminish the noise.

"Romeo Niner Five, I read negative sit rep, over."

I pressed the send button and once again whispered into the mouthpiece.

"Alpha Papa One, roger."

The radio fell silent. I pulled the blanket from my head and leaned back against the dike, laying the handset of the radio next to my head so I could hear any transmission immediately. The routine was all very by the book but calming nonetheless. Someone was out there in the dark, asking if everything was all right. They would be there, ready to help if the situation report was anything more than negative. It was comforting to know that wherever you went, or however bad the situation got, you were not alone as long as the PRC-25 radio kept working.

The radio was, indeed, the link to everything in Vietnam. The platoons carried the PRC-25 as a portable communications device that could reach the company and in some instances beyond that. Even when soldiers were in trouble and found their communications cut off, they could always reach the radio relay station on the fabled Black Virgin Mountain, called Nui Ba Den. It rose three thousand seven hundred feet on the edge of a flat plain and looked very much like a coffee pot on a pool table. Many battles had been fought to secure the top of the mountain so the 25th Infantry Division could place its radio relay up there. By early 1970, it was pretty much secure, although the soldier legend was that it had been overrun three times by troops of the North Vietnamese Army (NVA). Three times the entire complement of American troops up there were slaughtered. I never thought much about these stories until my last months in Vietnam, when I was assigned to—yep, you got it—Nui Ba Den.

I shifted position to peer over the rice dike, taking the starlight scope in my hands and switching it on. At the touching of my index finger to the power switch, a tiny electrical whine alerted me that the scope was on, and I looked through it. The world in the scope appeared as a montage of lime green Jell-O. The starlight scope was designed as a night-penetrating device long before the night-vision wonders of today. The starlight scope merely amplified available light, which was minimal at best, and made a green facsimile on the lens. It was big and heavy and generally useless, but we carried the thing anyway. I suppose any help is better than none when you are trying to see gremlins out there in the darkness. It was the carrying part that made us want to leave the thing behind.

The troops assigned ambush duty out of mechanized infantry companies did not have to carry food and all the things straight leg troops, or regular infantry, had to lug on walker missions. After all, we were the "Mech," and usually had the company circled up somewhere near us like a big, armored wagon train. What we did take with us, on those night jaunts, was only what was needed to wage battle. Each of us carried a weapon and about thirty magazines, two Claymore mines, twelve hand grenades, two hundred extra rounds for the machine gun, two star cluster flares, water, a rolled up army blanket, and sometimes the starlight scope or the radio. If you had personal weapons like a knife or a pistol, it added to the weight. When you consider eleven or so guys armed in such a manner and you add a machine gun and a grenade launcher or two, it is a pretty formidable group.

The ambush patrols were sent out to prearranged spots to intercept enemy troop movements under the cover of darkness. Army intelligence discovered where such enemy activity was most likely to occur and had infantry companies dispatch nine- or eleven-man ambush patrols to intercept the enemy. Experience would teach us that such interception was not always the best course of action.

At around 3:00 a.m., the clouds opened and the moon splashed a silver light across the dry, defunct rice fields. I was leaning back against the dike, sleepily surveying the open country behind us, when I felt something strike my right shoulder. I turned to see what it was and found an unfired bullet lying on the ground beside me. I felt the small thump on my shoulder again, and this time caught the round in my hand as it fell. I looked to my right and saw Oscar Solis waving at me. He had been throwing bullets at me to silently get my attention without moving from his position. I shrugged my shoulders and he pointed out across the rice field, then he held up both his hands opening and closing his fingers three times. It was a night signal indicating thirty men out in front of us. My hair stood on end and I hugged the ground, gently shaking Lester awake.

As we peered over the dike, we could plainly see the dark line of men moving slowly along the distant tree line. We could see them clearly in the moonlight, and we could see that Oscar had been mistaken. Everyone was now awake and silently counting. Thirty became forty, forty became fifty, and fifty grew into a nebulous number that filled us all with dread. We were nine, and just across the flat distance of the dead rice fields were who knew how many.

Clements was in charge of the ambush patrol that night. He crawled into a position between Lester and me and took the handset of the radio. In hushed tones he began to give direction and coordinates to the company, which would be passed along to the artillery. A moment or so elapsed and then Clements was talking directly to the artillery forward observer. With only a correction or two, everything was set and the word went down the line.

"Get low, boys."

The distinctive freight train sound of huge explosive shells going overhead caused us all to press our faces hard into the muddy earth and pray that the artillery boys were on the mark. The explosions tore the earth and split the night with ragged flashes of light. The screams of men crawled into our ears and made us shiver while the ground shook as if being stomped on by giants. Clements looked over the dike and adjusted fire via the radio. The second barrage seemed even louder than the first, and then there was silence.

Within a minute or two the air was lighted by artillery flares, and we looked across the distance with trepidation. We all knew what would come next. We would have to rise and walk across that open space and see what damage had been done. We would have to go where the remainder of a large group of enemy soldiers may have been hiding and waiting. All nine of us would have to do that.

Clements rose to stand on top of the rice dike and motion for us to get up. His shadow, cast by the light of the flickering artillery flare, seemed to dance on the dried ground before us. The image undulated like something out of a gruesome ballet. As we crossed the distance to the trees, I kept thinking, "I should have stayed in school. I should have stayed in school. I really should have stayed in school."

Track Four

CUE: *I Feel Like I'm Fixin' to Die,*
COUNTRY JOE AND THE FISH

Infantry school was a harried and completely serious cramming of everything deadly into the minds of those who were designated with the infamous brand of Eleven Bravo. The cadre personnel at Fort Ord were dedicated to giving us every edge we could possibly have before we were thrust headlong into the day-to-day confusion that was Vietnam. They tried, to the best of their abilities, to prepare us.

It was at Fort Ord that I first noticed the odd, arms-length kind of segregation that the rest of the army demonstrated toward the infantry. It was slight at first. We found that ladies at the PX and folks at the enlisted men's club would not look us in the eye if they could help it. It was easy enough to recognize infantry troops. We were made to wear the steel pot helmets everywhere we went. Not helmet liners, but the actual combat helmets. The practice had a practical application. It got us used to the inordinate weight of the headgear that we would wear on a daily basis in combat. It also singled us out and made it easy to know which troops had a really good chance of not coming home again. It was only the beginning of that odd discrimination we would feel from every other part of the army. When you graduated from infantry school, you were a member of the most elite, underpaid fraternity in the world. It was a club that almost no one wanted to be a part of, at least not in 1969.

Training stories are many and varied, but all seem to end with the same moral: a soldier may have to do every job on the battlefield, so we had to learn everything. We mastered every weapon and learned every technique they could teach without actually killing us in the process. It was their job, and they did it well. Now our job was to carry their lessons into the fray and be worthy of the task. It would be a tall order in my case. As it turned out, my religion was going to get in the way. I was a devout coward!

On December 5, I reported to the Oakland replacement detachment and entered the machinelike, moving mass of men who would be warehoused, reequipped, and shipped out within a few days. Before this experience I had no idea what a massive effort keeping the American presence in Vietnam really was. The entire place was teeming with men and equipment. They all seemed to be shuffling along in ever-moving lines and were constantly beset with seemingly endless reams of papers to sign. The whole business was housed inside a number of converted aircraft hangars that were absolutely huge. There

was row on row of bunk beds filled with men who seemingly stared up at the high, distant ceilings and the lights,
which never went off. Yes—the lights burned twenty-
four hours a day, making it extremely easy to become
disoriented as to the time or what day it was. The experience at the replacement detachment was something
each of us had to go through, and most endured it with
good humor. There were, however, those who did not.

There are all sorts of army stories. Most are reminis-
cences of duty and experience that recall people and
places with a certain amount of nostalgia. There are others that are simply not voiced because of the nature of
the moment and the feelings they impart when remembered. Those who worked as permanent personnel at the
replacement detachment in Oakland have more than
their share of these stories. Oakland was the place where
life in America and the reality of the war in Vietnam suddenly came face to face. It was the place where some lost
it entirely and ran screaming through that forest of bunks
and multitude of men in green boxer shorts. Under the
glare of those lights that never went out, some lost their
own inner light and were forever lost to us. The frequency of these sudden breakdowns would shock most of us.
Sadly, the personnel at the replacement detachment had
to deal with them, again and again and again. It is almost
mind-boggling when you consider that the war lasted
ten years. How many frightened and tortured souls did
they have to chase down through that mass of humanity,
knowing all the while that there would be more to
come? It must have been terrible duty, there at Oakland.

Fortunately, most who came through the Oakland station took the transition from a peacetime mindset to one
that would face the war with quiet acceptance. I am sure

that it has been that way for almost all troops awaiting embarkation. It was that step up onto the diving board, preceding a plunge into the water below. The time there was filled with anticipation and a great deal of uncertainty. That uncertainty would be lost when we found ourselves transported to Travis Air Force Base and placed on the jet that would start the twenty-one hour flight to Southeast Asia. I cannot remember much of what happened on the flight, but I remember the sound of the seat belt as I snapped it in place, in preparation for takeoff. I was leaving my homeland for the first time.

December is a wonderful time of year. All around the world, people are enjoying the winter weather and looking forward to the Christmas season. I must admit that my enchantment for snow and winter cold died an ignominious death when our plane landed in Anchorage, Alaska, and we all had to get out of the plane and stand on the runway. The snow was blowing in a thirty miles-an-hour wind, and we were all dressed in jungle fatigues, which were especially designed to keep you as cool as possible in tropical weather. It seems the army was worried that one of its new Vietnam-bound troopers might run away. It just goes to show the intricacies and ridiculous limits to which the military mind can be pushed. Who in his right mind would run off in the middle of an Alaskan snowstorm wearing clothes you can almost see through?

We were eventually marched out of the snow and fed breakfast. Afterward we were marched back out into the snow, where heads were counted to make sure we were all there. Then we stood, outside, in the snow, in our jungle fatigues, while men in insulated coveralls and wolverine parkas deiced the wings of the plane. As I said, I lost my love of winter somewhere on a runway in Alaska. I have never gotten it back.

The plane traveled across the Pacific, and much of that time is a blur to me. I suspect that I slept much of the way. I do know that at some time during the flight, we descended onto the tiny strip of land known as Wake Island. I remember that it was so small it looked like a cigar butt in the ocean when I saw it out the window. What I can't remember is whether it was on the way to or from the war when we landed there.

During the long transoceanic flight, I ran into Chester Johnson. He was from a small west Texas town near my home, and we had gone through infantry training together. We decided to sit together and spent many of the remaining hours swapping stories and confessing our dread about what was ahead. It was nice to have someone I knew in the seat next to mine. I have often wondered why no one else from our training company was on that plane with us. I did not realize it at the time, but there was a pattern unfolding that would set the Vietnam War apart from all the others. Soldiers came to the war not as part of a unit, but alone. Alone we came, to join units as the new guy, and after battle and time had carved out our place in the unit, we left. An order would come one day, and we would be gone, suddenly, and as alone as when we had come. We would be alone to make our way back home and reenter society, which had changed during our absence. No wonder so many had trouble making the leap back.

The jet swooped low, circling Mount Fujiyama, and then set down gently onto the runway. We were in Japan. We deplaned and, of course, the army counted heads to make sure we were all there. We were moved to another runway and made to stand in formation as another plane taxied up. The ramp came alongside, and we saw a large group of very tan GIs start moving off the plane. They were dressed in Class A khaki uniforms that were clean and pressed, but somehow the men themselves had a sort of rumpled look. Many of them whistled and yelled and pointed in our direction. Some seemed terribly reserved and smiled sadly in our direction. We knew, of course, that these were troops who had done their year and were on their way home from Vietnam. In essence, we were their replacements. As they got closer, it dawned on me that most of the men who seemed so reserved and had smiled sadly in our direction wore the crossed rifles of the infantry on their collars. They had a different look in their eyes. It was a look I would come to know well in the coming months.

The last leg of the flight was handled by a special airline that was contracted to make the flight from Japan to Vietnam, landing in areas that were sometimes under fire from enemy troops. The entire atmosphere was different from the moment we boarded the plane. The flight attendants tried to be especially attentive to each of us. I suspect they were spurred to this by two motivations. One was the fact that they had gifts and tips and souvenirs pressed on them by practically everyone. The other may have been the knowledge that there were young men in the cabin of that airplane who would never see home or an American girl again. Men began to unpin rank insignias and other military doodads and affix them to the uniforms of the flight attendants until those young women looked like something out of a comic opera, dripping with military junk.

"Gentlemen."

The voice was that of the pilot coming out of cheesy little overhead speakers.

"If you will look out the left side of the aircraft, you will see the coastline of the Republic of South Vietnam."

The entire plane fell silent, and most of the passengers on the right side of the plane rose and moved to look, with the rest, out the windows. Below us were sparkling white beaches leading up to a dense, thick growth of heavy forest that stretched as far as the eye could see. A soft murmur rose from a certain number of those who looked down on that thick undergrowth. I have no idea if it is true or not, but I would bet money that most of them were bound for infantry companies and would be fighting in those woods very soon.

The plane turned inland, and everyone took his seat. Two jet fighters came up on our left wing and hung there for a moment or two, then wagged their wings at us and veered off. I cannot remember if they were loaded with bombs or not. I was too mesmerized by the wooded nature of the landscape beneath us.

The pilot came on the speaker and told us to put our seats and tables in the upright position, and then the plane dropped suddenly from the sky and screamed onto the runway at Bien Hoa Air Base. We were there.

The plane rolled out and then began to taxi. It came to a stop before some tin buildings that looked very much like a wool warehouse in west Texas. Men were walking around on the tarmac, wearing green T-shirts and drinking cans of soda. No one seemed to be ducking bullets or running for a foxhole. In fact, I didn't see anything that even looked like a foxhole. Then the door was cracked open and air came in. It swarmed all over us like the breath of a large bakery oven. It had an odd,

mildew kind of odor and was so heavy with heat and
humidity that it literally took my breath away. A rather
tall sergeant, dressed in jungle fatigues, stepped into the
plane and held up his hand. Everyone fell silent. He
looked down the line of seats for only a moment,
checked something on a clipboard in his hand, and said,
"Good morning, gentlemen. Welcome to Vietnam."
Chester Johnson and I looked at one another and
solemnly shook hands. We quietly promised that we
would do so again a year later, on the way home. Oddly
enough, that is exactly what happened.

Track Five

CUE: *Born to Be Wild*, STEPPENWOLF

The heavy rumble of the diesel engine vibrated through my whole body. The blacktop ribbon of Highway Six Alpha stretched out before us, filled with military vehicles and the occasional civilian scooter. It seemed that the entire population of Vietnam rode some form of motor scooter or other. They even had small pickup trucks that were actually three-wheeled motor scooters with large beds mounted on the back. These small vehicles putted proudly along the highway and then took to the ditch when confronted by huge, olive-drab military monsters, such as the fabled "deuce-and-a-half" truck, so called for its two-and-a-half-ton capacity. When combat vehicles took to the roads in numbers, everything gave way to them. Such was the case this morning as the entirety of C Company, 1st of the 5th, ran along the blacktop on its way to the Ho Bo Woods.

The company comprised 164 men and 21 armored personnel carriers (APCs), including a medic's APC, a command APC, and a mortar platoon APC, and sometimes an APC repair vehicle. A full mechanized company like ours was pretty impressive in firepower. It boasted twenty-one .50-caliber machine guns, twenty or more M-60 machine guns, mortars, grenade launchers, M-16 rifles, hand grenades, knives, axes, shovels, and an unknown number of personal weapons, such as snubnosed pistols and Indian tomahawks. The mechanized infantry was the last remaining link with the old horse cavalry. As the army was changing its emphasis to Airmobile assault teams, the thoughts on cavalry tactics revolved more and more around helicopters and not ground-mounted troops, who rode APCs, tanks, or armored cars. This idea would be reversed as the United States faced ground warfare in the deserts of Iraq in the next century. In Vietnam, the APC-mounted soldier was a less-than-romantic figure when compared to the Air Cavalry of the day. The Airmobile boys were even allowed the luxury of jaunty cavalry hats right out of a John Ford movie.

The M113 armored personnel carrier was the backbone of the mechanized unit. The troops called it a "track" because it was a tracked vehicle, not unlike a tank. But tanks are heavily armored and support huge cannons for firepower. The armored personnel carrier is only "armored" on the back ramp. The rest is just a thick aluminum box that might deflect small-arms fire. It is armed with a Browning .50-caliber machine gun, which is nothing to sneeze at but is certainly no cannon.

During the Vietnam War, troops did not ride inside the tracks because of the danger of hitting land mines, which could breach the floor and kill or injure the troops inside. Instead, the soldiers rode on top of the track, on seats that were fashioned from hand-grenade crates or mortar-ammo boxes. The seats were actually a bit of a personal statement. Each man had his particular seat on the track, and he personalized it as he saw fit. I have seen everything from ammo crates to sawed-off desk chairs and even a helicopter seat. A man's place on the track was very important and had to be earned. If a man was wounded or killed, it was not unusual for his seat to go unfilled for a number of days out of respect, but then necessity and replacements came into play, and a new guy had to earn his spot on the top of the track. Every society has its rituals, I suppose.

The track was home, protection, and baggage cart to the mechanized soldier. Everything needed for battle and for existence was packed into or hung all over the track. To see a fully loaded mechanized company moving down the road must have been much like watching a Gypsy caravan in full flight. Guns, ammo, fence stakes, chain-link fencing, rolls of barbed wire, tarps, shovels, picks, sledgehammers, and water cans were visible all over the outside of the vehicle. The inside was stuffed with ammunition, explosives, C rations, and personal gear for the eight or so men who were riding on top. As I said, this was home to the mechanized soldier. We had no base camp barracks, nor did we get to go into the base camps much, except to get the tracks repaired. They shipped everything to us via helicopter, so we stayed out. We stayed out in places like the Ho Bo Woods or the Michelin rubber plantation. Our address was only a radio frequency, for we were constantly on the move.

A day in the Mech was long and often exhausting. That being said, it was still better than being in a straight leg unit. We were proud of the tracks and the fact that we could react to an enemy contact in only a few minutes, with tremendous power. Pride aside, it was still a long day.

The company was often called to reconnoiter certain areas that were suspected enemy strongholds. This meant long days, probing into forests or along river trails, looking for bunkers or signs of enemy movement. Generally such days turned up little and only burned another day off your tour of duty. Sometimes we turned up the enemy and were engaged in running gunfights until we either killed them or they slipped away. About four o'clock each afternoon, we circled the tracks up like a wagon train and began to build a mini-base camp of our own. We faced the tracks and their machine guns outward and stretched an eight-foot-high chain-link fence around the front of each track. This was done so that rocket-propelled grenades fired in our direction would explode on the wire and not on the track. We stretched two rows of concertina barbed wire around the entire encampment and then began digging fighting positions on either side of each track, filling sandbags to pile up around them. When all was ready, we had some time to rest and write letters and take care of personal necessities. During this down time, the platoon sergeant would come to us and pick the men who would go on ambush patrol that night. If you were picked, you got your gear ready and tried to sleep a little before it was time to go out. The longer you were in Vietnam, the easier it was to sleep on command.

At about 6:00 p.m., the ambush patrols would leave and make their way by a circuitous route to a holding site, where they would hide until about thirty minutes after full dark. When the sky was dark and the night was quiet, the ambush patrol would move silently into the ambush site. The men would deploy in a straight line or large "L" shape, lying on the ground or against the side of a rice dike, where they could cover the trail with rifle or machine-gun fire if the moment called for it. Each man carried a blanket, which he laid out on the ground. He would place himself and his equipment on the blanket so as not to make any more noise than was necessary. Each of us carried two Claymore mines, which were designed to explode and spread steel ball bearings in the direction of the enemy when set off. We would crawl out in the darkness and set up the mines, then string a detonation wire back to our position and hook up the klackers, which were the detonator handles. They looked very much like large green clothespins, but once squeezed, they caused death to fly into the night.

Once all was set up, everybody on the ambush stayed awake until midnight or so. If there was no action by then, the men would pair off, with one asleep and one awake until morning. If the night did not provide death and destruction, the sun would herald the time to return to the company site. The Claymores were rolled back up, and the blankets, which were now wet with either dew or rain, were also rolled up, and we would make our way back to the tracks. Once back in, we would report our findings for the night and take a little time to eat something out of the green cans that had become the main source of food to us. If the order was given to saddle up and move out, we tore down everything we had put up the night before and packed it on the track. We emptied the sandbags, filled in the holes, and climbed into our seats atop the track. The day was about to start all over again. There would be one day after another like this, interrupted only by a difference in orders or the incidents in which the routine erupted into enemy contact. In those cases, the day was often punctuated with blood and the realization that this war was a long way from over.

The wind blew through my hair this particular morning. My helmet was hooked over the edge of the .50-caliber shield. I hesitated to wear its weight any more than I had to. From my seat, just to the right of the gunner's hatch, I always had a clear view of the road ahead. I gained that seat when Sergeant Murphy got the "million-dollar wound"—the one that sends a soldier home—the very day I had come to C Company. It was mine by default on that day, but it became mine by right as the weeks went by. My seat on track 20, called the Two Zero track, and my place as a viable member of the squad had been won, and I felt as if I belonged.

Charlie Dunn sat in the gunner's hatch, to my left. Sergeant Dunn was Sioux, from the Rosebud Reservation, and was considered by all to be blessed by the Great Spirit. When Dunn had been leading ambush patrols, it was considered good luck to go out with him. Now that he was getting close to going home, he was considered a short timer. Because of this, he was made the .50-caliber gunner and did not have to leave the track at night. Since Dunn had been the squad leader on the Two Zero track, nothing had happened to any of us. It was whispered among the company that Two Zero was a lucky track. It was a rumor we did not try to dispel.

The speed of the company along the blacktop slowed, and we all checked our weapons to make sure they were loaded and the safety was off. We were approaching Trang Bang, which was often called the Viet Cong capital of the central highlands. There were so many enemy families in the village of Trang Bang that they often fired at us as we drove through. We sometimes turned the .50-caliber machine guns to the side and fired into the houses in response to sniper fire, but it seemed to have no real effect. In later years, Trang Bang would be immortalized in a Pulitzer Prize-winning photograph of a little girl running naked down a highway after being burned in a napalm attack. On this day, we were running down the road and had no time for monkey business with the locals.

We reached the cutoff point, and the company turned off the blacktop onto a well-worn dirt road. The tracks all pulled up in line, and the lieutenants dismounted and walked over to the command track to confer with the company commander. I find that I have a great deal of sympathy for those who were sent into combat with gold bars on their collars. They were the men in charge and had to act that way, even though they could be "new guys" to the fight, just like any replacement. It was easy enough to tell whether a new lieutenant was going to be a decent platoon leader or not by the amount of respect he gave to the experienced platoon sergeants. These non-commissioned officers, or noncoms, were the men who had run the war at the squad and platoon levels and had gained their rank and their experience in combat. If a new lieutenant came into a platoon and paid no attention to the platoon sergeant, he was dismissed as a flake, and side bets were made on how long he would last before he got himself or someone else killed. Second platoon was lucky. We were fortunate enough to have had two really good platoon leaders while I was with them. Lieutenant Kent Clark was one.

His name was actually James Kent Clark. It wasn't long before we discovered that and made quite a few jokes, playing on the fact that his name, backward, was Clark Kent. The Superman innuendos ran rampant for a few weeks, but after we came to understand and rely on him, the Kryptonite comments disappeared. Lieutenant Clark had actually been a peacetime sergeant in Germany who went to OCS and ended up leading a combat platoon in the III Corps area of Vietnam. His wife was worried sick the whole time he was with us. As it turned out, her worry was not without foundation.

Clark walked back to the 2nd Platoon tracks and informed us that we were to "RIF" along the edge of the woods in search of a possible VC bunker complex. "RIF" stood for reconnaissance in force. I'm not sure how much force can be attributed to a single platoon with only four tracks, but those were our orders, and we started off. We had made similar ventures along this same area several times. This one would prove to be different.

We dismounted and spread out in a loose line near the edge of the woods. The tracks drove in a slow line about fifty yards behind us, with only the driver and the gunner onboard. The rest of us began probing slightly into the wood line, looking for telltale signs of digging or tunnels. Three hundred yards along our path of search, Oscar Solis held up a hand and we all dropped low, watching him for signals. He moved slightly forward and peered into the dense underbrush, then made a signal by cupping one hand and running the index finger of his other hand through it. It was the silent language meaning he had found the entrance to a tunnel. Oscar stayed in place and Lieutenant Clark moved to his side. They spoke in hushed tones for a moment, and the lieutenant motioned for Lester and me to come forward. At that moment, the quick snapping sound of bullets passing overhead let us know that someone was shooting at us. We hugged the ground and tried to get a fix on where the shots were coming from. It was obvious that the fire had not originated from the entrance to the tunnel.

The heavy thumping sounds of the .50-caliber machine guns on the tracks suddenly began tearing up the wood line about fifty yards from our position. The track gunners had discovered the enemy, just as they were about to open up on us, and were pouring fire on them, giving us time to run from the wood line and take shelter behind the tracks. We began to make a steady withdrawal, keeping the VC pinned down with our machine guns until we were out of their rifle range. At that distance, our heavy .50-caliber guns could still keep them pinned down. A call was made, and within minutes, the shriek of jet fighters could be heard overhead. The jets made a sighting run, marking their targets with smoke rockets, then they turned around and came in low, dropping the oblong silver objects we recognized as napalm bombs.

As the jets screamed overhead, the woods suddenly erupted into a ball of fire. It was a fire that would grow on itself and feed on its own intensity. The pure horror of napalm is that it is a jellied gasoline. It sticks to whatever it touches and burns until the jellied substance is consumed or the oxygen is shut off from the fire. When dropped over tunnels or bunkers, the fire sucks all the oxygen out of the air to feed the fire. When dropped directly on any living thing, it sticks to the skin and cannot be removed until put out. Just the thought of it brings fear to the hearts of the bravest warrior, and yet its powerful results in stopping an enemy make it the weapon of choice in many situations. We had seen it save us on more than one occasion, and as we watched the woods burn with that hellish orange and black fire, we knew what would come next.

Enemy fire from the wood line had ceased. We remained at a distance with our machine guns trained on the far edges of the fire but expected no resistance. All we could do was wait for the fire to burn itself out and then check to see what was left. While we were waiting, a radio message from the company commander told us that one of the jets that had come to our rescue had been downed. The pilot had ejected safely, and we needed to pick him up. This was something new.

None of us had ever heard of a jet crashing anywhere near us. We thought it must have been some kind of mechanical malfunction. It seemed impossible that a few VC with only rifles could shoot down a Phantom jet. Whatever had caused it, there was a pilot on the ground, and the Two Zero track was sent to get him.

We first saw the bright color of the parachute. It was splayed out and rippling in the wind. The pilot was standing a few yards away, waving in our direction. We drove over and hauled him up onto the track. His eyes were wide open in a sort of adrenaline-induced euphoria, and he could not stop talking. It seemed something did hit his plane and cause it to flame out. Whether it was a stray bullet or a piece of his own ordnance, we would never know. He was so hyped up by the experience that he could hardly sit still. We radioed back to the company that we had picked him up and that he seemed none the worse for wear. Orders came back from the captain that we were to hang onto him and bring him in with us after we had finished checking the bunker site. He could go back in on the resupply chopper before dark. The thought of staying on the ground with us for a few hours seemed to excite the downed pilot even more.

When we got back to the rest of the platoon, the napalm fire was out. The first sergeant shook hands with the young pilot and then set up the group to go into the burn area to check for bodies. As we dismounted and checked our weapons in preparation, the pilot jumped down from the track and asked if he could go with us. The first sergeant shrugged and told us to get him a weapon and a helmet. In a few minutes we were making our way through the black ash, toward the place from where the enemy rifle fire had come. What would happen had become a matter of routine for us in the aftermath of napalm attacks. The area would be swept, looking for traces of the enemy who might have lived through the attack. Bodies that had burned were to be checked to make sure they were dead. If any survived and were still able to fight, they were to be taken or killed, whichever was their choice. The dead were never much more than crispy critters, and those who survived the fire were often so burned that they were hard to look upon. As we made our way through the burn site, the pilot fell quiet and eventually refused to speak at all. By the time we returned to the tracks, his face was ashen and he seemed almost incapable of communication. We gave him some water and helped him up onto the track, where he just sat and stared off into space.

That afternoon, when the resupply chopper came, the pilot was loaded onboard with two of our guys who were going home that day. They were excited and talking a mile a minute about home and what they were going to do, but as far as I could tell, the pilot never exchanged a word with them. As the helicopter lifted up and hovered there for a moment, I could see his face as he looked down on us. It was not the face of the daring young man who had fallen out of the sky. It was the face of a man who had seen, for the first time, what his contribution to the war actually caused on the ground. He had seen it, and he would never be the same again. As the helicopter blades bit into the air and turned toward the south, I realized for the first time the changes that had slowly overtaken me. It was not until that moment that I came to understand how desensitized I had become.

Track Six

Christmas 1969 was going to be different. Even the newest of the new guys could tell that. Since I had reached Vietnam in early December, I hadn't really given it much thought, because I figured I would be sent right away to a combat unit and would have other things on my mind by Christmas Eve. As it turned out, the route to the war had a turn or two in it.

After arriving at Bien Hoa that hot December day, we were hauled, by night, to Long Binh base camp. It was a spooky trip for those of us who were new in-country. Buses pulled up and we were shuffled on, only to notice that there was chicken wire over all the windows. When I asked about that, the driver replied that it kept the hand grenades out. I think it was about this time in my Vietnam experience that I stopped asking very many questions. The answers were entirely too disturbing.

We started out on the dark roads not really knowing what to expect. I suppose I expected to be taken to some small outpost in the middle of nowhere, surrounded by barbed wire and populated by hollow-eyed men in dirty green fatigues. That would come, but not yet.

Long Binh base camp was the third-largest military installation in the world. It was roughly the size of a small American city. The place had paved roads and electric lights and was the hub of comings and goings in South Vietnam. I was astounded that we had never even heard of the place. It certainly proved to be teeming with activity.

The group I was thrown in with was sent to the 90th Replacement Battalion. From there, thousands of men were dispatched to divisional base camps every day. In fact, there were formations six times a day in which line numbers were called out and the matching men shuffled off to find their place in the war. I assumed that I would be there only a matter of hours, but that was not to be my fate. When dawn came after that first long night, a sergeant came into the replacement barracks and called out everyone who was an Eleven Bravo. Here was the separation of the infantry in its purest form. A number of us looked about and stepped forward. We were marched to another barracks and informed that we were to serve as bunker guards at the replacement detachment. At this my heart gained a bit of undeserved hope. If we were to be bunker guards at Long Binh, it meant we would not be sent out into the fray with a line unit. My hopes were soon deflated when we were told this was only tempo-rary duty. We would be held at the replacement detach-ment for a sufficient amount of time to gather a new complement of fresh infantry faces to sit in the perimeter bunkers of Long Binh. Then we would be sent on to whichever combat unit needed replacements.

The time seemed to drag while we were on bunker guard. In fact, we had a rather odd schedule. We were on guard for six hours, then off for six hours, then on again. It served to exhaust and disorient most of us. I am not sure how long we stayed there, but my number was eventually called, and I was shipped to the 25th Infantry Division, at Cu Chi base camp. I would enter the war a bit late, but enter I would.

I remember the flight to Cu Chi as being amazingly short. We were loaded onto a C-130 airplane, which seemed to take off, rise up a little, and then land again—which is exactly what it did. Cu Chi and Long Binh are only about forty miles apart. We had been told we were going to the base camp of the 25th Division. In our minds, we all saw that deserted military outpost, surrounded by barbed wire and mines, that we had all imagined as the base camp in Vietnam. When the ramp of the plane dropped, we discovered Cu Chi was not as big as Long Binh, but it wasn't a frontier outpost either. It had huge runways, paved roads, and brick buildings. It was the nerve center of the 25th Division, and it took us a little by surprise.

We were loaded onto trucks and hauled off to the replacement depot, which had a sign on the roof bearing the image of Santa Claus dressed in shorts and a Hawaiian shirt and riding a surfboard. I had forgotten it was almost Christmas.

Time in the replacement depot was short and to the point. We were processed in and then separated out. Those of us who were blessed to bear the Eleven Bravo stigma were sent to "charm school." This was a short orientation on the local customs and what new threats were being found out there where the action was. At the culmination of the course, we were taken on a night ambush patrol somewhere outside the wire, just to get our feet wet. The ambush patrol to which I was assigned was uneventful, but two nights later, a charm school ambush patrol ran into a group of VC, and two of the new guys were killed in the fight.

When charm school was concluded, we were sent to a large gathering of wide-eyed new guys in the local amphitheater, which was built for the Bob Hope Christmas Show. We were all crowded into the area and handed sheets of paper with names and units listed on them. I received the paper and ran my finger down the list until I found my name and serial number. Beside my name was written "C Company 1/5 inf(M)." My first question was about the "(M)." I had never seen a military notation like that. It was of primary interest to me because it seemed to be where I was going. Someone bent over and whispered into my ear that it meant I was being assigned to a mechanized company. I was still in the dark until another brave soul explained that it was a cavalry unit, which rode into battle on APCs. I had seen the armored personnel carriers only once in training, but the thought of not having to walk all the time sounded pretty good to me.

We all sat down in the shade of that pavilion and waited. As I looked around I saw a familiar face. It was Rick Morris, who had been in my infantry training platoon at Fort Ord. I walked over to him and asked what his assignment was on the sheet. He grimaced and said he had been assigned to the 2nd Battalion of the 27th Infantry. This was a unit known as the 2nd Wolf Hounds.

The 1st Battalion of the 27th Infantry was, naturally, known as the 1st Wolf Hounds. Both units were legendary for combat bravado. Their unit motto was No Fear on Earth. This seemed pretty ridiculous to me, but then again, I was a devout coward and counted my lucky stars that I had been assigned elsewhere. Rick Morris expressed grim feelings about his assignment and was, in all likelihood, looking at a year of pretty rough duty, when the gods of fortune smiled at him.

While we were sitting there and bemoaning our fates, a first lieutenant in really clean fatigues walked up to Rick and said, "Aren't you Erik Morris?" Rick looked puzzled and said he was. Then the lieutenant explained that he had once worked for Rick's mother in California. He asked Rick what he was doing there, and Morris held up his unit assignment paper and said he was going to fight the war. The young officer scrutinized Rick for a moment and then said, "Maybe not." The lieutenant took Morris by the arm, and the two of them disappeared into the crowd.

I did not see Rick Morris again until my last few days in Vietnam. I encountered him in a snack bar in Cu Chi. It seems he had spent the whole year running the 25th Division snack bar. He had never been outside the wire and never fired a shot in anger. Rick Morris was saved from the life of a straight leg soldier in the 2nd Wolf Hounds by a chance encounter on the very day he was to be sent to a combat unit. All I could think of when I learned of this was that this must be proof there is a God.

Trucks began pulling up to the amphitheater, and calls went out for men who were assigned to this unit and that unit to climb aboard. I kept looking at the sheet in my hand and at the "1/5 inf (M)" next to my name. The crowd around me got smaller and smaller until there were only two of us left in the entire enclosure. I looked across the empty space at the only other GI left with a white paper in his hand. He looked back, and we started to move toward the middle. His name was George Bradley. He was stout and sweating from the heat and just as confused as I was. When we compared assignments, it became curiously evident that we were the only two guys in the 25th Division who were going to the 1st Battalion of the 5th Infantry (Mechanized) on that hot December day. Bradley and I sat down and waited. Just about the time we were contemplating desertion, a beat-up three-quarter-ton truck zoomed up and slid to a stop on the gravel. A tall, tanned sergeant in a bush hat and really faded fatigues got out and looked at Bradley and me.

"You men going to the 1st of the 5th?"

His voice was amazingly deep and matched his towering height. We both nodded in mute obedience and watched as he dropped the tailgate of the truck and motioned for us to get in. Once we were aboard, it was evident from the aroma that this vehicle was generally used to haul garbage. It seemed oddly appropriate at the time.

The 1st of the 5th had a small area reserved for it on the edge of the Cu Chi base camp. It included a small number of screened-in buildings surrounded by sandbags and mortar boxes filled with earth. The truth is that I don't know much more about it than that. Bradley and I spent one night there before being shipped out to C Company. Mechanized companies did not have barracks or even a place in the base camps. They lived and fought beyond the wire, like a great camp of armed nomads. At least that's how it was with C Company. I can count the times I saw a base camp on my fingers.

The next morning, Bradley and I were sent to the C Company orderly room. This was a semiscreened-in building from which the company clerk ran the entire war, or at least he seemed to think so. Actually, the role of the first sergeant and his company clerk cannot be underestimated in any war. Vietnam and C Company were no exception. These two men were the only ones in the entire outfit who knew where everything and everyone was at any given moment. It is a job that gets little praise but is terribly necessary. If an outfit gets a good clerk, it often protects and even spoils him in ways that would curl a general's hair. It should be said here that any general worth his salt had done the same thing for his clerk when he was a company commander. If he didn't, then he had hell to pay getting things done.

As Bradley and I entered the orderly room, we were greeted by Rosengarden, the company clerk. Everyone called him Rosie. We were signed into the company roster and given two beat-up M-16 rifles, which we began to clean so they would be combat ready. As we were sitting on the floor of the orderly room, scrubbing out the bores of those two tired weapons, I looked up and noticed a filing cabinet across the room from us. It had three drawers clearly marked with white cards that read "KIA," "WIA," and "MIA." I nudged Bradley and nodded in the direction of the filing cabinets. He took in the meanings of the letters on the white cards and then returned to his cleaning, without showing any emotion. I'm glad he didn't look at me. He might have seen the terror growing in my eyes.

Suddenly a breeze began to blow through the screen wire, and the slapping sounds of helicopter blades could be heard landing just outside. Rosie laid his body across his desk to hold down the loose papers scattered there. The door opened and in walked a tall man wearing no shirt and dripping blood from a compression bandage on his left arm. I noticed the blood spots on the concrete floor, which followed him as he walked to Rosengarden's desk and picked up the field telephone. He spun the crank on the phone and waited until a voice on the other end answered. Rosie asked him about a man named Murphy, to which the shirtless man replied, "Murphy's got the million-dollar wound."

A few terse words were spoken into the handset of the field telephone, and then the shirtless man turned on his heel and started for the door. The red spots splashing on the floor followed him.

"I'm going to the 12th Evac."

His voice had a smoky resonance to it, which struck me as amazingly calm as he walked out the door. I remembered the same tone in my father's voice when he was younger and in the Marine Corps.

The sound of the chopper blades picked up into a faster slapping cadence and then was suddenly gone. When silence again filled the orderly room, Rosengarden turned to us. He must have seen the confusion in our eyes, for without any real reason he said, "That was your company commander." My stomach rolled over a time or two, and I thought, "Oh My God! They're shooting the company commanders. What in heaven's name are they going to do to me?"

Two guys came into the orderly room sporting brand new haircuts and jungle fatigues that were faded from use but fresh from the laundry. Their tanned faces told us they had spent much time in the open, and the flat, emotionless look in their eyes was a hint of things to come.

They were Charlie Dunn and Jeff Hannah, two members of the 2nd Platoon who had been in the base camp for whatever reasons and were returning to the company. Bradley and I would look back on this day and our meeting with Dunn and Hannah as lucky, for we would go with them to the company and then to the 2nd Platoon. That, in itself, was a bit of good fortune we would come to appreciate.

We were loaded into a 548 resupply vehicle for the ride out to meet the company. The 548 is somewhat like an overgrown pickup truck on tracks. The ride to the edge of the base camp was dusty and uneventful, but it was a prelude to the tightening of our stomach muscles as we drove through the barbed-wire gates and swung out onto the blacktop of the highway. We were suddenly beyond the protection of the wire and surrounded by the people of Vietnam. They were everywhere, selling all sorts of wares from thatch-roofed stalls along the roadside and riding the ever-present motor scooters. The first thing that grabbed my attention was the fact that they really did wear those traditional pointy, wide-brimmed, straw hats.

As we entered the village of Cu Chi, I had my first true wartime awakening. There was a Vietnamese traffic cop directing traffic at an intersection. As we drew closer to him, I could see that he was standing with one foot on a body that was missing its head. I am not sure what effect that had on me, but the next sight sobered me quite a bit. As we moved forward, one vehicle at a time, I noticed that I could see a man staring at me, just over the little Vietnamese truck that was parked in the lane beside us. His gaze was intent, never wavering in the slightest. I tried not to stare back, but when I noticed that he seemed to have stalks of long grass clenched between his teeth, I simply could not help it. When the vehicle next to us finally moved forward, I came to realize that what I was looking at was the severed head from the body in the middle of the intersection. It was stuck on a spike, atop a garden wall. I must have turned a little green, because Charlie Dunn leaned over to me and quietly said, "They do that to prove that they are winning the war. It's kind of like a recruiting poster." Dunn was being kind to a new guy, but he wasn't fooled at all. He knew I was scared green, and he had the good manners not to say so. Hannah was not so empathetic. He looked first at me and then at Bradley before taking a long drag off his cigarette.

The first stop on our journey into the war was Fire Support Base Devin. Now this was exactly what I had pictured in my premonitions of the war. It was a small camp, surrounded by a circle of piled-up earth and coils of barbed wire, housing two large cannon and a few scared men who lived underground and peered out at the world through the ports of sandbag bunkers. What I didn't know was that we were bound for a war that had no fixed fortifications or permanent bunkers. Our home would be wherever we happened to circle up each afternoon, and our nights would be spent in forests, rice paddies, and rubber plantations. The eyes that peered out from the sandbagged bunkers of Fire Support Base Devin would watch us come and go many times during the next year. They would watch in silent understanding of the fact that some of us might not be back the next time.

We left Fire Support Base Devin in the 548 and started a trek along a narrow dirt road that led through small farming villages and ghost towns. We seemed to be get-

ting farther and farther from any form of civilization. I
kept wondering why there was no form of combat escort
with us. It didn't seem to bother Dunn or Hannah. In
fact, I don't think I saw them even look around us during most of the trip. When we turned off the slender dirt
road and took off across completely open ground, I
became a bit more than just worried. I saw Dunn reach
down and pick up his M-16, cradling it across his lap. It
was not until this very moment that it dawned on me
that I didn't have any bullets. Bradley and I had been
issued a couple of tired M-16s and one magazine apiece.
We were given no rounds of ammunition. As the 548
sped across the open ground toward a distant tree line, I
remember thinking that this was a hell of a way to enter
the war.

When we reached the very center of that open and
abandoned space, the 548 suddenly stopped. The driver
began throwing red mailbags over the side, and Hannah
and Dunn jumped out. Bradley and I looked at each
other and followed suit. We tossed our duffel bags to the
ground and jumped after them. It's a good thing we
jumped when we did, for before we hit the ground, the
548 was in motion, cutting a hard left in the muddy
ground and beating a fast retreat back to where it had
come from. The four of us stood alone and completely
exposed in the middle of South Vietnam. I was terrified,
Bradley was a bit irritated, and Hannah stretched out on
the mailbags to take a nap. He and Dunn both seemed
unperturbed that we had been abandoned by the US
Army in the middle of a war zone. I was, however, aghast
at the situation and was about to make my nervousness
obvious when an odd sound began to chip through the
wall of panic that surrounded me.

The sound was something like a combination of deep-throated mechanical rumblings accompanied by a chorus of really high-pitched chain saws. The others heard it too. Hannah sat up and pointed at the nearest wood line, where the trees seemed to hide the growing din. Then, as if suddenly flung from the depths of the forest, a line of armored personnel carriers burst out of the tree line and raced across the open ground toward our position. It was my first time seeing the spectacle of the mechanized forces in full array, and it was impressive. There were twenty-seven tracks in all, counting combat platoons, a mortar platoon, the angel track for the medics, and the command track. On this day, the company was also home base for two M-60 tanks, which were pretty impressive in themselves.

The tracks broke from the tree line in a single file but soon scattered into platoon-sized units and sped across the open ground four abreast. The earth trembled at their approach, and I could feel, as well as hear, the power of their engines as they reached the place where the four of us stood. As if by silent command, they began to move in a wide arc until we found ourselves surrounded by large, olive-green machines that belched diesel smoke and kicked up dust. Bradley and I stood in dumb amazement as the tracks sped around us and took their positions in a huge defensive circle, not unlike that of a wagon train, but with each track facing out.

The men aboard the iron monsters appeared to be a diverse group. They were deeply tanned and covered with dust, a fact that became more evident as many of them removed their sunglasses, exposing skin that was not powdered with trail dirt. It seemed that almost the whole outfit wore either sunglasses or goggles. It was an affectation that made them look rakish and hid from view the tired eyes behind those dark lenses. There seemed to be no standard uniform. Most were dressed in faded jungle fatigues, but many wore olive-drab T-shirts, and some had no shirts on at all. They jumped from the tracks and began the many tasks necessary to turn the circle of APCs into a night defensive position, or laager site. Each man seemed to know what was expected of him and moved from task to task without direction.

The first sergeant was standing a few yards from us next to the command track. He spoke to several young lieutenants and then turned his attention to the mailbags and the new guys. He stepped over to us and stuck out his hand. Eager to make a good impression, I shook it, and the older man looked at me and shook his head.

"That's real friendly son, but what I really need are your orders."

I blushed and fumbled in my duffel bag for the sheaf of papers that I had carried out from the orderly room. I handed them over and he glanced at them.

"Sweatmon. That's you?"

I nodded.

"What do they call you?"

"Stoney."

The older man looked at me and then back at the paper. "It says here, Robert B."

I swallowed and shifted my feet. "That's right."

He looked up at me and then off at the army of men who were sweating to put the laager site in order.

"I suppose there's a story behind that, but I don't have time for it. All right Robert B. that they call Stoney, do your job, keep your nose clean, and your ass down. We'll get along."

The first sergeant stepped past me and reached for Bradley's papers. He looked down at them for a moment and then back to size Bradley up a bit.

"Bradley, . . . George, is it?"

Bradley squared his shoulders and spoke with a steady voice. "That's right."

"All right, George Bradley, what do they call you?"

Bradley cut his eyes at me and replied in a voice that had a slight edge to it, "George Bradley."

The first sergeant smiled and looked back down at the papers in his hand. "Refreshing," he quipped. "You two go with Dunn to the 2nd Platoon. Welcome to C Company."

The two of us followed Charlie Dunn over to the place where the 2nd Platoon had parked its tracks. In the dim reaches of my memory, I don't think Dunn ever looked at us. He simply stopped by the Two Four track, dropped Bradley off, and moved on, leading me to the Two Zero track. This would be my home in the months to come. The men who rode Two Zero would become my closest associates, yet on this first day, none of them seemed to pay me much mind. As the months wore on, I would come to understand this detachment. It was a natural reaction to new guys. It was not meant personally or as any kind of insult. It was simply a part of the natural insulation that must surround the infantry soldier. It was a fundamental fact of war, but on that first day, it made me feel very much alone.

As the sun set that first night, I climbed on top of the Two Zero track to look around and take in my situation. I had finally come to the place I had been anticipating. I was in the infantry, in a war zone, a long way from any civilization. I was wearing the uniform of my country and carrying a weapon, and I would be expected to use it. As the dark enveloped me, I was completely aware that if I was lucky, I had a year of this to go through.

As I stood there in the gloom atop the track, Dunn climbed up and sat down in the gunner's hatch. He lit a cigarette and leaned back, observing the darkness before us. "You might as well sit down," he said in his quiet, calm voice. "It's going to be a long war, and you won't make such a good target." I sat down on the hand grenade case next to the gunner's hatch. It was a place that would become mine as time went by, but on this night it was an uncomfortable seat in the middle of an uncomfortable war, and I remember wishing that I was anywhere else but there.

I am reminded that there is an ancient warning that tells us to be careful what we wish for.

Track Seven

CUE: *I'll Be Home for Christmas*, FRANK SINATRA

As I have alluded to previously, Christmas seemed miles away and much out of place to me in December '69. The temperatures soared well over one hundred degrees, and my new assignment with Charlie Company was occupying most of my thoughts. We were working the edge of the infamous Ho Bo Woods, and I was trying hard to become a successful combat soldier. That means, of course, one who stays alive. Despite all this concentration in the wilderness of Southeast Asia, Christmas found us.

I can't remember exactly what day it was. I think it was the twenty-third of December. At any rate, we were ordered to stand down for the day, and we moved the tracks into Cu Chi base camp. When we got in, we were ordered to secure all weapons and load up on a series of deuce–and–a–half trucks. The trucks drove us to the area of the 25th Division amphitheater. As we neared the place, we began to see line upon line of men walking in that direction. We saw jeeps and trucks parked in solid files along the roadside. As we got closer, we saw thousands of men, stretched as far as you can imagine, trying to get a sight line to the distant stage. The odd part was that no matter how many men were stacked up, hundreds of yards from the stage, we kept moving forward. In fact, we drove right up within a few yards of the stage and were ordered to get off the trucks. MPs who were standing there led us to a line of empty seats in the third row from the stage. There was a sign there that read, "C co 1/5 (M)". As we sat down, I noticed similar signs all about us. Each sign reserved close seating for a combat-line unit. It was suddenly evident that the combat troops were being given first priority. This was something to which they were unaccustomed, but in that place it was the rule, not the exception. For the next few hours, we would be under the command of the most influential and respected man in all the US armed forces. We were there at the behest of Bob Hope.

I had grown up hearing tales of Bob Hope and his legendary efforts on behalf of the men and women who put themselves on the line for our country. My father had flown part of Hope's troupe around the South Pacific during World War II and had watched his Christmas show at a snowbound Marine Corps airfield during the Korean action. I had watched his televised Christmas shows from military bases around the world and had always found myself emotionally touched by this man's efforts to bring a little bit of home to those who were serving their country in so many far-flung places. On this day, as Hope walked onto the stage before a crowd of thousands who sat sweltering under the tropical sun of a land far from home, I felt as if I were suddenly connected to all those who had spent Christmas in war zones and away from their families over the years. This very good man had given up all those Christmases with his family to be with us and many others just like us, and at that moment he could have asked us to march barefoot to Hanoi and end the war. Believe me, we would have done it.

Hope was his usual wisecracking self, the girls were gorgeous, and the music was a touch of home that many of us had not had time to think about. It was absolutely wonderful, and was over entirely too soon. As the whole audience sang "White Christmas" along with the cast, we were reminded how far away home really was and how far these people had come to share the moment with us. It was kind of sobering, and then it was over. We had been the first in and we were the first hauled out. We went back to the company area and were soon on our way back to the Ho Bo Woods. The war was still there, right where we had left it.

The next day was fairly easy. We did some road duty, which included running north and returning with a convoy of trucks, and moving the company into a new night defensive position. We had to string all the wire, fill all the sandbags, and dig all the holes. Once set up, we had to fill the roster for night ambush patrol. I was lucky: I did not have to go out on Christmas Eve. Those who had been chosen went about their preparations with the silence that preceded any ambush. It was different in only one way: each of them seemed not to want to look into the eyes of another soldier. They seemed lost in thoughts that were probably very far away and filled with loved ones who were not a part of that hot place in Asia. As they left the wire, I watched them go. I watched and noticed that no one in the group looked back. It was unusual.

Darkness fell and the stars came out. Vietnam was a place that was often swathed in clouds. The humidity often covered the skies with wispy layers that hid the constellations from those of us who slept in the open every night. Christmas Eve, however, was clear. I sat on top of the Two Zero track, watching beyond the tangle of concertina barbed wire. I had the first watch, but very soon I wasn't alone. One by one, the other members of the squad climbed up to take their places on the track, and we began talking of home and Christmas. It was an odd conversation, but one that seemed completely appropriate on that warm December night. Each of us told Christmas stories of home and family, and somehow it seemed to draw us closer together.

At midnight, something happened that struck each of us deeply. In the distant night sky, we could see the lights atop the radio relay station at Nui Ba Den, known as the Black Virgin Mountain. The mountain was far enough away that the lights appeared as a constellation in the night sky, a tiny ring of bright stars that floated in the celestial darkness. At the stroke of midnight, flares began to appear in the sky around the peak of the mountain. Red, green, and white star clusters began to explode in the air until the mountain appeared to be a volcano spewing bright, Christmas-colored lights out into the night sky. It was an astounding sight and seemed to go on forever.

You could hear the voices of men all around us in the dark, calling their comrades to come and see this sight.

We all sat mesmerized by the light show in the sky until the last flare burned itself out and left the night dark, clear, and filled with God's stars. Then we could hear a soft male voice begin to sing. I have no idea who the singer was, but the song was unmistakable. It was "Silent Night." Almost as if they had been called to do so, other voices in the darkness began to join in, until many voices were singing the simple melody. As the last notes of the song were reached, the voices got softer and then were gone. Silence reigned for a moment, and then the loud and commanding voice of Sergeant MacAdams cut into the dark silence.

"Keep your eyes open and your mouth shut! Merry Christmas."

In the years since that night, I have often been asked about Christmas memories. I have been asked about my favorite Christmas memories, which I tell. I have been asked about my happiest Christmas, and I tell of that. When I am asked about my most memorable Christmas, I recall Christmas Eve 1969, and usually say nothing at all. I wonder if those who were there and are still alive have the same feeling.

Track Eight

CUE: *Like a Rolling Stone*, BOB DYLAN

The dull report of the blast caused everyone to look up and then get down. When the smoke rose over the berm of piled-up earth, we all realized that the explosion had come from just inside the perimeter, and then shrill calls for a medic rose through the afternoon heat. As we grabbed for weapons and started for the fighting positions, the word came that it had been an accidental explosion, not an enemy attack. Each man seemed to release himself from the tension that precedes combat and slowly crawled atop the defensive mound of earth, which surrounded the fire-support base. From that vantage point, I witnessed the first death of a comrade in arms. It was a tragic and almost textbook accident that took the life of "Tex" White, and yet it drove home the importance of the rehearsed precautions of handling the tools of warfare. It was a hard-won lesson that may have saved lives in the long run. Certainly it made each of us painfully aware of the destructive power we lived with and carried each day.

Raymond White was from Victoria, Texas. He was proud of his home state, proud enough to use the name "Tex" among those who knew him. It gave the two of us something in common, which was big medicine in an army unit. On the morning before his untimely death, I took a photograph of him standing on the back of his track, proudly displaying a Texas state flag that was attached to the radio antenna. It would be the last picture ever taken of Raymond White.

The Claymore mine is a superb defensive weapon. It is a small, lightweight contraption about two inches thick, six inches wide, and about a foot long. It is filled with C-4 explosive and buckshot. To operate this handy little gadget, the soldier must unfold the legs that are on the bottom of the mine and stab them into the earth. A blasting cap, which is attached to a twenty-five-yard-long extension cord, must be screwed into the top of the mine. This can be set off by pressing a clacker that is plugged into the other end of the extension cord. Until this is all assembled, the Claymore is relatively harmless. The C-4 explosive is amazingly inert until charged by heat and fire at the same time, such as the detonation of a blasting cap. This is how infantry soldiers can carry the mines and even engage in combat without much fear of explosion. The trick is not to have the thing all hooked up until you are ready to use it. On this particular morning, Tex White seemed to have forgotten that rule. He seemed to have been carrying a Claymore that was armed and ready to go when the explosion took place.

No one will ever be sure why he was doing that, or what caused the mine to detonate. It was enough to know that it did.

I stood on the defensive berm and watched the medics running to the place where the smoke still hung. The body of Tex White was split almost in half, and there was no sign of life. The others about me soon turned and went back to what they had been doing before. They made no mention of what they had just seen. It was a strange and almost surreal moment. A moment I would eventually come to understand. I had joined a family that had its own customs and rules of deportment. This distancing of the horrifying, and in some cases the inevitable, was a protection of sorts. It kept the thoughts of what might be from playing a larger role than mere possibility. Raymond White would live on in our thoughts, but his name was never again mentioned in connection with that incident while we were in-country.

The war went on as if there had never been a Tex White. We loaded up and moved out on some form of mechanized mission or other. I can't remember what that might have been. Life in the mechanized infantry came to be like one long road trip on which the scenery changed along with the mission, but the purpose was always the same. I have often wondered what it must have been like to be assigned to a straight leg unit or a rear-echelon company, where each soldier had a bed and a locker and some place to call home. Even the ground infantry units had a headquarters and a barracks, or "hooch," back in the base camps. The mechanized or cavalry units made their home with the tracks. Wherever the company set up for the night was the current address, and each man thought of the particular APC to which he was assigned as home. The fact that sometimes as many as eight men were assigned to a track made the conditions a bit crowded.

Each replacement soldier came to the company with a duffel bag filled with fatigues and socks and the like. The bag was thrown into the track along with machine-gun ammunition, explosives, C rations, and all the other necessities of life in a war zone. Each day it was all packed and unpacked and piled up beside the track, as the promise of night drew near. Each man finally came to the realization that the duffel bag was only good for holding laundry and spare clothing. Everything else that was considered personal could be kept in an empty .50-caliber ammunition can. Every man had a can that was marked with his name and treated as if it were a safe-deposit box at a bank. No one else touched your box, and the same was expected of you. Inside the very personal green can was kept money, letters, pictures, and all sorts of items that were important to its owner. It would have been amazingly easy to steal from so many unlocked personal safes, but I cannot remember anyone ever complaining that they had been robbed. Maybe it was simply not a good idea to take from men who carried loaded weapons with them everywhere they went. We called such thinking machine-gun logic.

Because the tracks were quite small inside, there was usually sleeping room for only four men. Two would sleep on the narrow benches that stretched out on either side of the track's interior. Two men could sleep on medical stretchers, which were hung from straps attached to the ceiling. Everyone else had to find someplace to sleep outside, on the ground. Some of the squad members were out on ambush patrol each night, and someone was always on guard on top of the track, so that left only a few to curl up in their blankets somewhere outside the track. The really strange thing was that you got used to it.

I remember one incident when Lester Lorig and I were flown into Cu Chi for a citation ceremony. We had been out on ambush for several nights running and were really exhausted. They showed us into a screened-in building that was completely empty. They said we could hang out there until the general arrived. We took off our gear, laid down our weapons, and curled up on the concrete floor for a nap. You have no idea how comfortable that smooth floor felt to both of us. There were no rocks or tree roots digging into our sides, nor was it wet or muddy. I remember thinking, just before I dropped off to sleep on that hard concrete floor, that I had been out in the bush entirely too long.

The only other thing that was considered the personal property of each man was his combat equipment. These were the tools of our trade and were customized and prized by each man individually. The odd fact was that most of the stuff was handed down from one man to another as they left the platoon for one reason or another. The war in Vietnam lasted ten years for the American troops. Many of the companies had been in the field for years on end and consequently, some of the equipment was years old when we got our hands on it. It had served another soldier before you put it on for the first time, and each man secretly hoped some luck would accompany the equipment of a veteran.

On the first night I was picked to go out on ambush patrol, the guys of the 2nd Platoon took much care in dressing and equipping me for the experience. It was not unlike a matador being dressed before the bullfight. I was given the pistol belt that had belonged to Sergeant Murphy. It was the same Murphy who had gotten the million-dollar wound the day Bradley and I were sent to C Company. I would not know until much later that Murphy had hit a mine, which took his knees out. The guys didn't mention that as they were decking me out for combat.

The pistol belt went around your waist, and on it hung several things you might need. A canteen for water was placed back on your hip. Two empty canteen covers were placed on either side and filled with hand grenades. Two flares were shoved into the belt, one green and one red, in case you needed them. If you chose to carry the short army shovel, which was called an entrenching tool, it was hung on the back of the belt. The standard weapon of the war was the M-16 rifle. If you carried that weapon, then an empty bag for a Claymore mine was hung over your shoulder and filled with thirty loaded rifle magazines. You were given two belts of machine-gun ammunition for the M-60 machine gun. These were toted either in a box with a sling or draped naked over your shoulder like Pancho Villa.

The last touch was the army blanket. Actually, the army had devised a lightweight covering for outdoor sleeping and the like, which was perfect for the Asian climate. It was called a poncho liner and was so light it weighed almost nothing. It also could dry out in a very short time after being drenched by rain. It was wonderful and perfectly adapted to our situation. Unfortunately, almost none of these wonderful items ever reached the field. They were confiscated by troops in rear-echelon positions to cover their bunks in dry, comfy barracks buildings, or were turned into jackets on which Vietnamese embroidery proudly stated that they were going to heaven because they had spent their time in hell. It was one of the bones of contention between the line troops and the men who served in the rear. We carried wool army blankets, tied up with boot laces, rather than the lightweight poncho liners that were supposed to be part of our equipment. When they hung this wool monstrosity around me on the afternoon before that first ambush patrol, I was simply told, "Don't ask."

The steel helmet each man wore was a billboard for personal expression. It was covered with a camouflage-colored material, which became adorned with all sorts of messages and artwork symbolizing the taste and attitude of the wearer. It was much like nose art on the aircraft of World War II. Everything from peace symbols to calendars were printed on them. Sometimes personal messages were displayed that took some explanation or knowledge of pop culture back in the United States for a clear understanding. My favorite was on the helmet of Charlie Dunn, who was from the Sioux Nation in South Dakota. The message on his helmet paraphrased the popular Johnny Cash song "A Boy Named Sue." It announced, in large, Marks-A-Lot letters, "I am a Sioux. How do you do? Now you gonna die!"

On my helmet, I stenciled my cattle brand from back home. The elastic band that circled the helmet and served to hold items like a toothbrush bore my army handle of "Stoney." It was, in my case, a link to my old life and the hope of returning home. I wore that helmet until one particularly bad night when it became lost in the shuffle. After that, I picked up one that had been worn by Joe

Raber, which had a bullet hole dead in the front of it. He had come away unscathed and kept the bullet and made a necklace out of it. He was not so lucky a second time. He was wearing that bullet but not his helmet the day he was shot in the head and killed. I kept the helmet until I left the company.

Weaponry was also somewhat personal. The average platoon had a certain number of weapons issued to it and it was expected to keep those weapons. It was, however, a peculiarity of the mechanized troops to keep and use a number of personal weapons. I was no exception.

The M-16 was the standard infantryman's weapon. It was light and easy to operate and amazingly adapted to close combat. It did, however, seem to have some problems in the jungles of Asia. There were all sorts of horror stories about the weapon jamming and leaving troops defenseless in the middle of firefights. I have no idea how true those stories were, but it did happen to me. The weapon quit working in the midst of a really nasty encounter, and I began not to trust it. As fortune would have it, I ran across a lieutenant who was from Texas and was on his way home. He had purchased a tommy gun from a soldier in the Army of the Republic of Viet Nam (ARVN). Those guys were notorious for selling everything that wasn't nailed down, and some things that were. The lieutenant had bought the tommy gun but could find no magazines for it. He had never fired it and saw no chance of getting home with it, so he sold it to me for sixty dollars.

I was ecstatic. I had a World War II tommy gun, which was tough as a boot, would operate in the worst conditions, and shot .45-caliber pistol ammunition. It was a match made in heaven. My father sent me the magazines for the gun, all the way from Texas, and I was in business. It was one of those personal quirks that made the mech soldiers so different. We carried all sorts of personal weapons along with the standard stuff issued by the army. If we were to be the stepchildren of the 25th Infantry Division, at least we would look the part. As the time wore on and we began to feel more and more isolated from the rest of the army, we became more and more attached to the company and each other. I suppose misery loves company. I am eternally thankful that the family we forged was made up of such amazing and admirable individuals. I came to know these men when things were absolutely at their worst, and I discovered an undeniable truth: men are at their best when things are worst.

Track Nine

CUE: *The Ballad of Davy Crockett*, THE WELLINGTONS

A hand shook me awake. The darkness seemed thicker than usual as I rubbed the fatigue from my eyes. The wages of so many nights on ambush were beginning to take their toll on us all, and that night, on me in particular. The hand shook me again, and the wheezing whisper of Dennis Kinney let me know that this was not a dream, or at least if it was, it was a part of the same nightmare we all were sharing.

"Stoney." The sound of my name brought me around a bit faster. "We're moving."

The realization of Kinney's words sunk in and caused me to sit bolt upright in the darkness. Moving an ambush after it was already set was tantamount to suicide. If the VC didn't already know where you were, the thrashing around of nine, night-blind guys through the underbrush should draw the attention of anything that was within earshot.

I crawled out into the darkness to retrieve my Claymore mines. The others on the ambush were doing the same thing, making a sort of hushed rustling in the leafy undergrowth. It was actually very quiet, when you consider that nine guys were crawling around on their stomachs, trying not to make much noise and keeping as low as possible while retrieving and packing their equipment. It was relatively hushed, and yet every sound in the darkness raised the hair on the back of my neck. Soon we were packed and standing in a ragged line, feeling extremely naked in the gloom. Lieutenant Phillips came down the line until he reached the spot where I stood. Lester and I were usually the last ones on the end of the line of travel. It was our responsibility to keep a lookout behind us as we moved through the bush. On this night, I was alone in that duty. Lester was not there for some reason. Phillips looked beyond me into the darkened woods and then tugged at my sleeve. He leaned close and whispered the kind of thing no one wants to hear on a black night in Vietnam.

"Battalion says that there is huge movement about two clicks up ahead of us. They want us to go have a look."

I wanted to blurt out, "Are they nuts?" What actually came out was, "You're kidding," and I swallowed pretty hard when he said, "No." He slapped me on the back and turned to go but came back and whispered that I should keep a pace count. I nodded dumbly and began, once again, to think of all the reasons I really should not have been there.

For those uneducated in the strange and wonderful ways of the US Army, some explanation might be helpful. In this not-so-atypical example of true army procedure, some guys back at the base camp had gotten a report, from who knows what or whom, that there was a rather large group of enemy soldiers moving along the edge of the Michelin rubber plantation under the cover of darkness. Our little nine-man ambush patrol was the closest American contingent to this reported enemy line of march. This being the case, and the army thinking like it thinks, we were ordered to pick up in the middle of the night, find our way through the rubber trees for two thousand yards or better, and eyeball this force. We were to make our way along unknown ground, in pitch black night, being silent as death and trying not to run into any enemy ambushes or stumbling into the very troops we were supposed to be sneaking up on. I was not elated as I began to calculate our chances for success. This was not the first time we had been sent to scope out a larger enemy force, and it left me with the definite impression we were considered expendable by someone.

As we began a careful advance into the deeper darkness of the rubber trees, I looked behind us and then began the tedious task of keeping a pace count of our journey, all the time wishing that Lester Lorig was there. It was he who usually kept the pace count with me and was amazingly accurate under many a dire circumstance. Between the two of us, we could generally be fairly close when it came to measuring distance. This night, I was counting alone.

The pace count is one of those amazingly bright army schemes in which, in this case, a man is supposed to know how long his stride is and be able to translate that into the distance he has traveled by foot. This technique is taught on army bases, which have many a rough terrain to practice on. The only things they don't include in such training are really dark nights, filled with booby traps, land mines, people who'd like to shoot you, and guys like me who were filled with just plain old-fashioned fear. When you add that into the mix, the accuracy of the pace count becomes mythical at best and nonsensical most of the time.

We moved out through the darkness and I began to count. Almost immediately, Kinney fell over a log directly in front of me, and I stepped on his hand. He whispered obscenities and punched me hard on the right knee, then struggled to his feet and followed after the dim shadows that marched on ahead of us. I limped after him, trying to remember where I had left off in the pace count.

Some three hundred yards later, everybody fell on their faces in the leaf-covered ground under the rubber trees and held their breath. In the distance, a light could be seen bobbing through the regimented stand of trees. We lay silently, watching as the light seemed to float through the darkness with an unsteady pace. It seemed as if it was headed straight for us. Each man brought his weapon to bear and waited for what would come. I fingered the trigger of the tommy gun and thought to myself that the light ahead of us must be the beam of a small flashlight in the hand of someone unaware that we were even in the vicinity. It must have been that, for just as suddenly as it had appeared, the light vanished. It vanished as if extinguished on purpose, to hide the position of its bearer. The rubber trees were once again bathed in perfect darkness, and we lay on the ground, waiting and watching for whoever might have held the light. When we were fairly certain that no one was in front of our line of march, we rose and started out again. I had completely forgotten where I was in the pace count, so I estimated and started up again. I was positive it didn't make any difference.

As the group drew closer to the intended target of our march, the ground grew less and less hospitable. We lurched over fallen trees and stumbled into sunken ditches filled with water. We tripped over tree roots and were slapped in the face by low-hanging branches that were invisible in the blackness. It was at this point that I remembered a sergeant's parable that said the most dangerous thing in a combat zone was a second lieutenant with a map and a compass. On this night, with young Lieutenant Phillips leading us bravely through the darkness, I was hoping that parables were not always right.

We stopped three more times in anticipation of discovery by enemy ambush patrols. Each time was a false alarm, and each time when we started forward again, I was more and more confused about the pace count. Finally we stopped and stood quietly under the rubber trees. Lieutenant Phillips came back to me and inquired about the distance we had traveled. I had to say something, so I just made it up. I told him that the hardstand road we were seeking should be about a hundred yards ahead. The truth was that I had no idea how far we had to go. An even stranger truth is that we walked one hundred ragged paces and stepped right on that paved road, exactly where I said it would be.

No one was more surprised than I was. The lieutenant came back and told me what an outstanding pace count I had made, under amazingly hard conditions. We set up in the bushes just south of the road and watched until morning. We never saw a soul. The whole thing had been for nothing, but the story about my amazing pace count made its way around the company. Rumor had it that I was the illegitimate son of Davy Crockett, who could follow a mouse trail across the Grand Canyon on a dark night. It was all pretty stupid when you remember that I had no idea how far we had really come that night. Les Lorig knew better, but it is to his credit that he never gave me up. He just made sure that his pace counts were always right when we had to count together. It got us where we were going and saved my unearned reputation as a frontiersman.

Track Ten

CUE: *Mama Told Me (Not to Come)*, THREE DOG NIGHT

One of the sad connotations of almost all Hollywood depictions of the Vietnam War has been the insistence that the drug culture invaded the military in general and the combat units in particular and led to a complete breakdown of anything that even looked like discipline or effectiveness on the part of the Americans in Southeast Asia. Scriptwriters, seeking easy plot devices, seemed to find a plethora of semipsychotic characters and morally corrupt situations to make the war seem reprehensible and just plain horrible on the screen.

Actually, such detours into the fictional dark side of man's nature were, as always, completely unnecessary. Combat veterans from Gettysburg to Iwo Jima would all stand in one long line, if they could, and insist that all wars are reprehensible and just plain horrible. The very fact that Hollywood types want to add something to the mixture to make the whole experience more vivid to an audience announces to the veterans of such battles just how little is understood about the true nature of combat. In the case of the Vietnam War movies, lack of intelligence and moral decadence seem to be the lynchpins of character, as far as the average soldier is concerned. In my own experience, I found nothing to be farther from the truth.

By the latter months of 1969, the United States found itself in the midst of a genuine revolution of ideas and actions. Politics was evolving at an alarming rate, demonstrated by the upheaval that followed the presidential election of 1968. The youth of America seemed bent on blasting out a place in history that was completely theirs, despite the negative legacy it might leave. From this frayed tapestry of the American experience came the soldiers who would carry the flag into battle in the infamous conflict known as the Vietnam War.

Every American serviceman who served in the now-defunct Republic of South Vietnam went there branded with one of four prefixes to his serial number. I have already alluded to the importance and the stigma attached to the Eleven Bravo designation of infantry troops. The prefix of the army serial number has to stand second in line as the mark that defined a soldier in Vietnam, at least to his comrades in arms.

Every serial number was preceded by the letters RA, US, or NG. All officers had the letter O before the series of numbers, but they were not a part of the stigma game, for they were all either products of Officer Candidate School, Reserve Officer Training in some college, or the United States Military Academy at West Point. This being the case, they were all volunteers by some method or other, and by that very definition were considered somewhat lacking in common sense by most of the enlisted ranks. It is an age-old prejudice, which I am sure was born among those who followed Alexander the Great halfway around the globe. It is the avocation of all enlisted soldiers to find ways to look down their noses at the officers who lead them into battle, even when they admire the leaders. In C Company, we were lucky enough to have had a few who were that admirable.

The letters RA preceding a serial number indicated regular army. Simply stated, this meant the bearer of such a serial number had walked into a recruiting office and offered himself up for the good of the nation. He was a volunteer. He was a man who had joined the service of his own volition for an enlistment of three to six years. He often had the choice of what kind of training he would take and what his primary military occupational status would be. That being the case, many of us marveled at the RA types who ended up in the infantry, in a combat zone. Possibly this is why the RA in a man's serial number was often defined as "real ass." Having said that, I need to confess that some of the bravest men I have ever met had volunteered to stand with us in that hot and awful place, halfway around the world. I have no idea what possessed them to voluntarily take such a terrible risk, but I will be eternally grateful that they did.

The letters US preceding a serial number indicated the soldier in question had been drafted. It meant he had been plucked from his life back in "the world" and given no choice in where he would go or what he would do while he served his Uncle Sam. It is no wonder the majority of Eleven Bravo troops were designated as US in their serial numbers. Most of the men in rear-echelon jobs or who were still back in the United States were RA by designation, and all of the senior noncoms were RA. That's because the enlistment of a draftee was for only two years. To reach higher rank required reenlistment, thereby converting him to the ranks of the regular army. For those of us who had been drafted and dragged off into combat, the US before our serial numbers stood for "unvoluntary servitude." No matter how grammatically incorrect that might be, it was true enough.

The letters NG rarely showed up in Vietnam. When it did, a certain amount of pity went with it. The letters stood for "National Guard." This should be self-explanatory but actually is not. National Guard units are actually state militia groups back in the United States. Such units have, from time to time, been activated to serve as part of the US Army during war. This was true in World War II, when such National Guard units served proudly and gained much well-earned praise. It would not be so in the Vietnam era.

As far as I know, no National Guard units served in combat during the unpleasantness in Vietnam. However, any number of National Guard soldiers volunteered for service there. Generally these were senior noncoms and officers who wanted combat credits on their record so as to gain promotion before they retired from the service. It was a last-ditch effort to get a buck or two more in their government pension check, which was not possible without service in a war zone as a part of their resume. When this was the case, the NG types were held in especially low regard by almost everyone concerned. They were often referred to as "f——— NGs." The name was sometimes richly deserved.

C Company, 1st of the 5th, was an amazing cross-section of America. It was a microcosm of young men sent into harm's way by the troubled times and, in some cases, by their own design. The educational level spanned a wide spectrum, from those with college degrees who had run out of time on the infamous 2-S deferment, to those who had simply run out of time. Actually, the educational level seemed a bit higher in the 2nd Platoon, probably just by the luck of the draw.

C. L. Clements was the platoon sergeant and a sort of guru for the rest of us. He already had a bachelor's degree and was working on his master's when the draft finally caught up to him. He was a philosopher and a leader and a nonreconstructed pacifist who found himself neck deep in the war he so adamantly disagreed with. He was a solid soldier and a many-times-decorated fighter who was one of the many who stepped up to the plate when he was called.

Gilreath, Perc McCaa, Dunn, MacAvoy, and I had all spent a couple of years in college before circumstances exposed us to the draft. I'm sure there were others with college hours, but for the life of me I can't remember who they were. The rest of the platoon was made up of skilled craftsmen and farmers and a general representation of the vocations that held up the world from nine to five in the America that was our homeland. There was even Hal Greer, a trumpet player in a small band deep in the southland. We had been plucked from all over the American continent and thrown together in a small and intimate group to face the fortunes of war as a cohesive unit. It would become a unit that lived and fought separately from the rest of the army, and for that very reason we came to regard each other in a special way. As the days stretched into months, keeping the company out in the field without ties to a base camp, we lost any thought of what was going on in the rear areas. We became isolated and completely dependent on each other. The platoon and the company would become our only world. In this way, social problems that had drifted into the base camps from back home in the United States skipped over us entirely. When such worldly problems caught up to Company C, it would be in a way that took lives and left a mark on our hearts that still has not healed.

For those of us who spent day after day in the field, drugs were simply not available. We spent almost all our time in what were called free-fire zones. These were areas in which we were the only friendly concentration of troops. In such an area, the only people we encountered were labeled as the enemy. The local VC were not too interested in risking a bullet in the butt just to sell a little pot to some dope-smoking GIs. There was no supply, so there were no dope smokers. At least there were none that I ever knew about. Long missions in places like the Michelin rubber plantation or the Ho Bo Woods didn't give us much chance to rub elbows with the natives or buy their wares. Needless to say, the Hollywood depictions of dope-smoking parties with soldiers sitting in sandbag bunkers that were decked out with Christmas lights and centerfold cutouts from *Playboy* magazine is something I never encountered. We needed to be able to count on each other when the chips were down. It would stand to reason that dope smoking would play hob with that type of responsibility. It was not a part of life in the field.

I did come in contact with exactly that experience when I was sent to a rehabilitation center in Cam Ranh

Bay following my stay in the 12th Evac Hospital in Cu Chi. There was a stretch of beach there where the convalescing troops could sit on the sand and watch night fall over the ocean. On a section of that beach some gathered and segregated themselves racially, black and white. It was the first time I encountered such a social distinction in the army. It was unheard of in infantry companies and especially in C Company, 1st of the 5th. There a man was judged by his deportment in combat. There were no colors, save the red of blood, and every man bleeds red. I was quite taken aback by this obvious racial tension in the base camp of Cam Ranh Bay, and a little surprised when I detected the acrid smell of marijuana smoke hanging over the two groups gathered on that beach. Perhaps my protracted stay in a mechanized combat unit had rendered me naïve to the times. If so, it was naiveté born of the necessity to trust the man next to you at all costs. I was never disappointed or let down by any of the men I served with under fire.

Track Eleven

CUE: *For What It's Worth*, BUFFALO SPRINGFIELD

The sharp snapping sound just overhead caused me to hug the ground as if I could melt into the damp earth if I tried hard enough. The thick darkness enveloped us completely, hiding our numbers and our movements from the eyes of those who would stop us. The cloak of night was our best friend, but it was also a terrifying equalizer during nocturnal encounters in unfriendly territory. These were the days before infrared goggles and night-vision glasses. At the time, the gloom of night favored those who knew best how to use its invisibility, and too often that proved to be Victor Charlie—the Viet Cong.

The snapping sounds came again, and I rolled over on my back to see that the tracer rounds, which split the dark above us, were red. Red was the color of the tracers used in American machine guns or those of the ARVN, which were supplied by the Americans. The shots splitting the air just over our heads were from friendly weapons. I crawled on my back up next to Lester, who was on his back as well. In whispered obscenities, we discussed the possibility that we had stumbled across another ambush patrol that was unaware of our presence in the area and were firing at what they thought was a group of VC.

The others, who lay behind us in the darkness, began to stir. We could hear the voice of someone on the radio attempting to make contact with the company. The hushed voice was trying to explain the situation in flat, whispered tones. When a hard slapping sound ripped the night air above us, the power of the whiplike concussions and the lime-green color of the tracer rounds explained the situation all too well. Green was the color of communist-issued tracer bullets. We were prostrate on the ground, smack in the middle of a firefight between American and NVA forces.

My pulse began to thunder in my ears as the realization set in. The rush in my temples seemed to pound harder as some of the rounds flying overhead struck limbs of the rubber trees and showered us with leaves and pieces of bark. The impact of the bullets was higher up in the trees than I had anticipated. In fact, they would have missed us if we had been standing upright. Lester raised his right hand into the darkness as the rounds cracked overhead. I thought he had lost his mind, but his gesture made it clear to both of us that the shooting was not low enough to hit any of our group. It eventually became apparent that they were not shooting at us. We were simply pinned to the ground, in between the two antagonists, who seemed totally unaware of our presence. The issue was whether to try to move out from under the line of fire or simply wait it out, without getting shot in the process.

After what seemed like an eternity, word came down the line in muffled whispers that we were going to try to crawl out of there. There was the chance that our side might call in artillery to suppress the heavier enemy machine-gun fire, and we might just get caught in the middle of all that. Moving was a gamble, but staying might have been an even bigger risk. My mouth was really dry, and I pulled out my canteen to get a sip of water when the shooting stopped as suddenly as it had begun. The silence hung in the inky night and became almost louder than the shooting had been. Fate had taken a hand. We could not chance a move now. We had no idea where either side was hiding, nor which way they might move in the darkness. Our very survival depended on our not being discovered by anyone until sunrise.

We seemed to have been trapped in a slight depression in the ground that was large enough to house the entire group. It's possible the very nature of this dish-shaped area was what had made the line of fire so far above us. At any rate, it provided a modicum of cover for the group, and so the nine of us circled up and faced outward, not knowing from which direction trouble might come. The hours passed and we strained our ears for any telltale sound in the gloom beyond us. I don't know about anyone else, but I never heard a thing.

Sometime in the early morning, Lester and I began to spell each other so we could get some sleep. I took the first turn, and he rolled up in his blanket, cradling his weapon in his arms. During that first watch, the moon rose over the rubber plantation, and the thick darkness was washed away by the soft glow of silver light, shining through the trees and making odd patterns of night shadows on the ground. You would think that being able to see was better, but on this night, I felt as if the cloak of darkness had been pulled from our shoulders and we were laid bare for the eyes beyond the trees to discover. I looked down the line of our defensive position and could see each and every one of us clearly. My stomach sort of rolled over as I realized how vulnerable we were.

The night passed slower than most, but as the sun warmed the eastern sky, each of us was awake to see what kind of fix we might be in. The early morning light revealed the faces I had not been able to see in the darkness. Gilreath was peering intently over the breech of his M-60 machine gun, sweeping the tree line with the intensity of one who hopes there is no bogey man just over the horizon. Dennis Kinney was just to the left of Gilreath. His eyes were bloodshot from lack of sleep and darted back and forth as he peered through the trees, trying to see some sign of what had kept us penned there all night. Lester was quietly cleaning his glasses, which were constantly filmy in the Asian climate. Each man held his position and waited for what would come in the morning light.

Two hours of bright sun failed to produce even a single hint of a combatant from the night before. Finally, the lieutenant rose from the ground and motioned for us to follow him in the direction from which the green tracer bullets had come. We walked warily through the stand of rubber trees, only to find that no one was there. They had pulled out sometime during the night. We made radio contact with the company and asked about the friendly forces that had shot over our heads in the darkness. We stood around under the shade of the trees while static-filled responses told us no one had been reported in the area by higher authority, nor had there been any reports of an action with the enemy during the night. It was all as if it had never happened.

As we carefully made our way through the regimented lines of rubber trees back to the relative safety of the tracks, I was struck by the absurdity of the whole situation. Here I was, thousands of miles from my homeland, engaged in a war that was not of my choosing, serving with men who were similarly trapped in the foibles of the times, returning from an armed incident in which even the players couldn't tell the players without a program. At that moment, the World War II acronym *snafu* took on a new meaning, and I felt a strange kinship with every man who had ever shouldered a rifle or followed the flag. I am sure that at one time or another, they all felt what I was feeling at that moment. As we entered the circle of tracks and made our way back to the 2nd Platoon, we were asked again and again, "What happened?" Lester and I simply shrugged. The truth was that nothing had happened. A whole lot of nothing had happened. How do you explain that?

Track Twelve

CUE: *This Train*, PETER, PAUL, AND MARY

As long as soldiers have been marching off to war, there have been those marching with them who came to comfort them by the tenets of their religion. The ten years of warfare in Vietnam were certainly no exception. The army chaplain has become something of a legend in the American military. It is completely humbling for those of us who entered the fray armed with the best that technology and the taxpayers' money could give us to know there were those who came armed only with their faith and the pure intention that no man should face death without the comfort of God nearby. Military chaplains are a breed unto themselves, but the minister who carries his pastoral duties into the battlefield should share a special reward in heaven. At least that is my opinion, and I dare to say it is an opinion shared by generations of combat soldiers. These are very special men.

I can't imagine how hard it must be to stand in a pulpit at an army base and preach the gospel of love and peace to those who are being readied to take as many human lives as possible in the interest of their country. I suspect that the congregations are a bit restless and even skeptical in such safe and militarily regulated environments. I do know that the attitude and the acceptance of the faithful changes somewhat when the cathedral is a shaded grotto in a combat zone and the thought of being closer to God is only a bullet or two away.

The mechanized units must have suffered somewhat from a lack of spiritual guidance. Since we had no barracks or home in the base camps, the sky pilots had to come out to us. They were a complete and ready-to-play traveling show. All they needed was a lift on the next helicopter bound for glory and they were ready to go. The whole premise is pretty admirable when you consider that they were coming out to stay with us for the night no matter what was going on or how high the possibility was that we might make enemy contact while they were with us. I never heard one of these men of faith complain or even hint that he would rather be somewhere else.

I can only remember one time we were actually hit while a chaplain was out with us. He was a black Methodist minister who had a completely disarming smile and was just plain huge. He should have been playing nose tackle in the National Football League, but instead he was guiding the souls of the faithful in the middle of a very unpopular war. On this particular night, we received rocket-propelled grenade fire into the circle

of the tracks, causing injury and carnage in the darkness.
I remember looking out of my fighting position and seeing his huge frame, running across the laager site, lit by
the weird and pulsating light of the parachute flares
above us. I thought he was running for cover but had to
revise that opinion when I saw him return, carrying the
limp figure of a wounded soldier in his arms as if it were
a small child. The following day we stood before him
with heads bowed, trying not to look at the fresh row of
helmets hung on upside-down rifles that were stuck into
the ground by the bayonets at their muzzles. His voice
was calm and even soothing as he read the service for the
dead. I can still hear his voice. It was a rich baritone, with
the throaty resonance that only black ministers seem to
possess.

"Ashes to ashes, dust to dust, in the sure and certain
hope of the resurrection unto eternal life, through our
Lord Jesus Christ."

I don't believe I ever saw him again. I don't think I
would know him if we bumped into each other on the
street, yet the timbre of his voice on that overcast morning so many years ago is etched in my memory. I am not
sure what drives a man to the service of his faith. I suppose there are many versions of what they term the call
to the ministry. I have been skeptical of such dedication
in cases of evangelists who seem to make millions and
live like kings off the fruits of their calling. I have been
convinced of it in cases of simple men who give their
whole lives to the calling, sometimes having to work
extra jobs to support their families while they give of
themselves, without reservation, to the faith. I have been
awed by the sheer miracle of those who enter the battle
without weapon or defense of any kind, bringing the

strength and comfort of faith to those who are sent into harm's way. These are truly special individuals, and I never met one who does not still hold my utmost admiration.

Track Thirteen

CUE: *Somebody to Love*, JEFFERSON AIRPLANE

The blades of the helicopter made that flat, slapping noise that became the signature sound bite for the Vietnam War. It was something we all took for granted at the time. The helicopter was the main manner of transport for supplies and replacements to those of us who lived in the field. For the straight leg units, it was the taxicab to battle. But on this particular day, the sounds of the slapping prop and the wind that bit at our faces was something rare. We were being airlifted for a walker mission, which was a bit out of character.

We had moved the entire company to a place near a low group of mountains that were within spitting distance of the Cambodian border. After the tracks circled up, the word went around that men were being picked for a walking mission. That was not good news to anyone. We were principally cavalry troops and were used to going out at night for a short walk and a long ambush patrol, but the thought of walking for days and carrying everything on our backs was not a pleasant one. It was too close to what we had all been trained for, back in the world, and we all thought we had put that kind of foolishness behind us when we were assigned to a mechanized unit. Obviously we were wrong about that. In fact, we were slowly but surely becoming aware of the fact that much of what we had been told by the powers that be in the US Army simply could not be counted on. This mission would not do anything to dispel those thoughts.

As the lots were cast and most of the 2nd Platoon was picked to go on this mysterious jaunt, an officer we had never seen came to inform us of new ground rules for this chess game. We were told that we were simply to go where the lieutenant would lead us and quietly observe any movements of the enemy we might happen to see. We were not to make contact of any kind if possible, and if we were forced into a combat situation, we were to break off as soon as possible and make our escape. We were not to take anything personal, such as letters from home, which might give any more information about us than the cryptic notations that were stamped on our dog tags. At this point, those of us who had been around for a while began to squirm a bit.

After the unknown officer with the bad news left us, we gathered around Lieutenant Phillips and began to ask all sorts of questions, which he couldn't answer. All we knew was that we were going to be flown to parts unknown and dumped out to wander around and look for hostiles whom we were forbidden to fight with. We were troubled by the fact that the maps given to Phillips were of an amazingly small area and had no indication as to latitude or longitude, which could have given us some idea of the location.

And so there we were, loaded up on Huey choppers, flying along to parts unknown, and carrying a heck of a lot of combat equipment we were ordered not to use.

As the choppers began to lose altitude, we could make out a rather large river below us and realized that a huge section of the riverbank was on fire, with smoke billowing up into the atmosphere. Cobra gunships were prepping the landing zone with rockets and fire from their miniguns. This was a five-barreled Gatling gun that delivered three thousand rounds per minute on the chosen target. To have the Cobra team as a backup in combat was a blessing. On this day, each of us looked at the column of smoke rising in the air and secretly wished the Cobras had found some other place to play. They were advertising our landings to every enemy soldier in the area.

The choppers began to stage for landing, and we began to prepare to disembark the helicopters as they hit the ground. This was usually a very smooth and very quick operation, however this time the ground was covered in thick, smoldering ashes from the fires that had been set by the Cobra gunships. As the helicopters reached the ground, the downdraft of their blades sent up a black dust storm of microscopic ash particles that obscured all vision and blinded everyone who jumped from the helicopters to the ground. We made our way out of this maelstrom by grabbing onto the pack of the man in front of us and trying not to breathe in any more of the fouled air than necessary.

How the chopper pilots kept from hitting other helicopters or flying straight into the ground is still a mystery to me. They had to be as blind as the rest of us, but they kept coming and going, until the sound of their props faded in the distance and the cloud of black ash began to dissipate. We squatted on the hot ground, shifting from one foot to the other, trying to keep from being burned by the still-glowing embers, which stretched as far as we could see. I have yet to understand why the higher-ups decided to smoke the ground of our landing zone like that. I am sure there was a military reason for it, but to the eyes of a simple soldier, all it did was waste ammunition and let everyone within miles know something was going on at that particular spot. There was another consequence.

As the choppers departed and we began making our way through the burned landscape, we found that the heat of Vietnam was intensified by the smoldering ground under our feet. This was no trivial thing. We were lugging heavy rucksacks loaded with all the food and ammunition we might need for the next three days or so. It was a load that added to our distress at the heat and was particularly overpowering to the new guys who had not been in-country very long. We began to lose them to the heat before we could make it to the river.

There was one new kid who was simply not well chosen for the infantry. He was extremely young and terribly fair skinned. He was so pale that his hair seemed almost white. To make matters worse, he had only been with the company for a couple of days, so he hadn't really had much chance to accustom himself to the heat in the field. Sadly, it caught up to him while we were making our way through the smoldering ground on our way to places unknown. His eyes rolled back in his head and he collapsed, right there on the black ash.

The medic came up the line to look at him and told Lieutenant Phillips that the boy would not make it through the next few days. The only choice we had was to call back one of the choppers for a medical dustoff.

Lester and I were picked to carry the kid back to a clear spot where the helicopter could come in and pick him up. As we reached the clearing, Lester threw out a red smoke canister to mark our position, and the aircraft began to descend. The closer the helicopter got to the scorched earth, the more it kicked the powdery ash into the air. Soon there was a black hurricane surrounding us, making it impossible to keep our eyes open, much less see. We were blind, crouching in the swirling ash, holding the limp body of the pale kid.

We started trying to pick our way forward, inching through the thick ash cloud, using the sound of the helicopter's prop as a heading. The closer we got, the harder the ash seemed to hit us, until our faces and arms were stinging from the blinding assault. Suddenly, two hands reached out of the swirling ash and grabbed my arm. The door gunner from the medevac chopper had walked out into the ash storm and was guiding us in. He was wearing a flight helmet equipped with an eye shield, and he looked like an alien from a spaceship. When we got to the helicopter and loaded the kid, the gunner turned to us and made signs that we should lie flat on the ground. We did so as the helicopter blades picked up their rhythm, and soon the storm of ash got even worse. Our ears and noses were filled with black particles as the helicopter blades bit into the air and began to lift the machine into the sky. The shock of the prop wash beat our clothes and forced the ash under our eyelids, pummeling us until the craft had enough altitude to pitch forward and be gone.

Lester and I lay in the ash until we could see once more. The ground was almost hot enough to burn through our clothes, so we got to our feet. Spitting and swearing, we began to retrace our steps back to where we had left the others. We were covered in soot, and when we made our way to the river, we washed our faces. Then we joined the others in considering how and where to cross the water.

The river crossing took about half an hour, and then we were once again on our way through the rambling forest. The quiet was not unlike the stillness we had known in other parts of the III Corps area, but there was something different about it. One of the things we noticed was that there was never a sound beyond that of a natural wooded area. We had become accustomed to the sounds of Vietnam. There were often aircraft high overhead, or even the sounds of artillery in the distance. There were the spattering sounds of Chinook helicopters on their way to resupply some unit, and sometimes even the high-pitched engines of the artillery spotter planes that cruised for hours over some places. Sound traveled a long way, in the quiet that was often Vietnam, but it was rare that a whole day produced none of the sounds of a military campaign in full swing. In this place, as we made our way through the trees and bushes, there were only the sounds of the forest.

An hour or so into this walk in the sun, the point element breaking the trail signaled for us to get down, and we all went into combat mode. Lieutenant Phillips came back to the end of the line, where Lester and I were lying in the grass. "I think we have a trail," he whispered. "Why don't you come take a look?"

It took me a moment to realize that he was talking to me. I had forgotten the Davy Crockett reputation that my bogus pace count had gained me back in the Michelin rubber plantation. I looked at Lester, who nodded his head and then looked away. I will never be sure how he kept from laughing out loud, but he managed to stay silent.

I followed Phillips up to the front of the line, where he showed me several footprints that looked as if they had been made before the morning dew. I had grown up in the ranch country of west Texas and knew a few rudimentary things about nature and tracking. I knew that men walking made the grass lie down in the direction they were going. I knew that dew drops in a footprint meant that it had been made before the early morning hours. I knew that deeper heel prints meant that the maker was hauling a heavy load, but when I saw these footprints, I knew we were looking at something altogether different.

There was a steady line of clear tracks that were made by smaller feet but of different sizes. The men who made these tracks were all wearing the same type of rubber-soled shoes. Off to the right of the footprints were small tire tracks, probably made by bicycle tires that had dug deeply into the soft ground. It didn't take Davy Crockett to read this sign. It meant we had crossed the trail of the regular North Vietnamese Army. The local VC would not have all been wearing the same shoes, and the bicycles meant these guys were probably carrying more equipment than they could lug on their backs, so the bikes became equipment haulers. Added together, these dis-

coveries meant there was a large regular army unit somewhere in the area, and these guys were part of their supply unit.

Phillips came forward and kneeled beside me. He
wrote with his finger in the damp earth, forming the letters N V A, and then a question mark. I nodded and
checked the Thompson to see if it was cocked. Somehow
the stakes had gotten a bit higher with our discovery. We
stayed there a moment while Phillips made some notes
on the map he carried, then we silently made our way
back to the rest of the group. Phillips motioned for us to
move out, and we began to make our way through the
shaded growth of the forest once more. This time we
moved in absolute silence, using GI sign language when
communication was necessary. We realized we were in
the enemy's backyard. The only question seemed to be,
where was this backyard?

That night we came to a spot on the top of the cut
bank of a small creek. Someone had been there ahead of
us. We knew this because there were already foxholes and
two-man fighting positions dug there. From the looks of
things, they had not been used for some time, but we
found old mackerel cans and some trash left behind. That
meant whoever had been there had stayed long enough
to make a trash pile. The fact that there were no C-ration
cans in the refuse told us that this had not been an
American camp. It also told us that whoever had been
there was not at all nervous about anyone knowing about
their presence. This was not the usual routine of the Viet
Cong, who survived by stealth. Whoever had been at that
place was guarding it for some reason, and they were not
trying to hide from anybody.

As soldiers tend to do, we began quietly talking among ourselves about the situation. There was something odd about the whole mission. There were plenty of leg units in the 25th Division. Why pull a bunch of mechanized troops off their tracks and send them on a walker mission? Why all the secrecy about the maps? We had never before been given maps showing only the immediate area. Why were we not engaging in regular radio traffic with the company? We were making contact only twice a day, and they were not calling us at all. We had come across signs of the enemy but done nothing about it. We had not even called in the discovery. When I talked quietly with Lester about it, his opinion was based on the distance traveled and the river we had crossed. In a flat, whispered tone that bore no emotion at all, Lester theorized that we were no longer in the Republic of South Vietnam. By his calculations, we were eleven men wandering around in Cambodia.

I don't think I slept much that night. I kept going over and over the thought that the US Army had picked me up and dropped me into another country. If it was so, then we were invaders in a nation in which we had no status as a protecting force, no other troops to back us up, and no allies. If we were in Cambodia, then we were in the middle of the Ho Chi Minh Trail and the stomping ground of the North Vietnamese Army. My mind kept going over these possibilities and pressing me with a question: What were we supposed to be doing in Cambodia? I had no clue.

The next day we made wide circular sweeps in three directions. During one of these arcs, we stopped to take a break. Everybody took off his equipment and stretched out. I was going to catch a nap when Lieutenant Phillips came over to get me. He wanted to check out a noise he had heard just ahead of us in the thick woods. I grumbled a bit and then got up, taking only the tommy gun, a bag of magazines, and a few hand grenades with me. I was still kind of sleepy as I walked beside Phillips along a slender trail that wound through the trees. Oscar Solis and Dennis Kinney walked just behind the lieutenant and me. I stepped off the trail, remembering that it wasn't a really good idea to travel along trails in strange country. The whole group did the same, and we began to meander through the trees. It seemed Phillips had no real heading in mind as we moved along. We stopped periodically, listening for the odd noise and moving along again, until we found ourselves frozen in our tracks by the unmistakable hiss of a shortwave radio being tuned. We stood stock-still in the trees while the sound came to us on the breeze. It was clear as a bell, and then it was gone.

We stood for the longest time, holding our breath and straining to hear any hint of the mysterious sound, but it never came again. Finally, Phillips shrugged and then whispered to me, "OK. Better take us back in."

I was completely stunned. I had been following him. I thought he had been taking us somewhere in particular and I was just walking sleepily along with him. Suddenly it was startlingly clear that Phillips had been under the delusion that I was leading the group. He was so wrong, but I had to admit that I had come to understand the meandering route we had been taking. I took several deep breaths and tried to gather myself, hoping I could remember even a little of the path we had taken. The forest ground was covered in shadow and a thick blanket of fallen leaves, and I was the first to realize that my finding our trail back to the place where the others were hiding and waiting for us was a pretty slim prospect.

I turned us around and began walking in the general direction whence we had come. If we were truly in Cambodia, we couldn't risk any sound or calling out for a heading. We had left the camp without taking a radio with us, so that kind of communication was not possible. If we missed the rest of the guys, we could walk all the way to the Mekong River before I actually knew where we were. The farther we walked, the more I was sure that I had no idea where the others were waiting for us, and I felt my ill-gotten Davy Crockett reputation melting away with every step.

When I had walked far enough that even I knew we should have come across someone, I stopped, leaned against a tree, and tried to think of some way to tell Lieutenant Phillips that Davy Crockett was lost. The others sat down for a break and seemed completely calm in the thought that I was leading them home through the forest primeval. At that moment, I saw a motion through the trees about fifty yards to my right. It was a miracle. Through the low-hanging limbs of the trees, I could just catch sight of a familiar face. Larry Grubbs had stood up and was stretching his muscles. Then I saw Lester move into my sight line. The whole group was roughly fifty yards or so to my right, and I could see them through the leaves and limbs of the Cambodian woods. They both sat back down and were gone from my sight, but I knew where they were. It had been a chance moment that saved the lot of us. Had we not stopped, and had I not looked to my right at just that moment, we could have walked on past them and been a footnote in history today.

I made a wide circle through the brush, with Phillips and the rest walking behind me. We went into the camp from the rear, and all was well. Phillips came to me and said he had become a little disoriented out there. He confessed that when I made the turn in the woods, he had checked his compass and was about to ask me what I was doing, when we walked into the other guys. "I was worried," he said, and patted me on the back. "But I should have known better." I don't think he had any idea how close he came to being listed among the missing.

Our odd mission lasted only three days. At the end of that time, Phillips made some notation in a little book he carried and scribbled on the portion of the map that showed where we had been, and we started back. We never saw anyone. We didn't fire a shot. When we got back to the tracks, the whole group of us went to Phillips and asked him where we had been. He looked at us for a long moment and then looked at the ground. "I really don't know," was his choked reply. I think it was the only time he ever lied to us. I think it bothered him more than he realized to do so.

In early May, we crossed the Mekong River into Cambodia as the spearhead of a general invasion along that border. The move was announced by President Richard Nixon and observed by the viewing public on network newscasts. For most of the world, it was a new chapter in the saga of the war in Southeast Asia, but for eleven of us from the 2nd Platoon of C Company, 1st of the 5th (Mech), it was a move over familiar ground.

Track Fourteen

CUE: *The Legend of Wooley Swamp,*
THE CHARLIE DANIELS BAND

There is much exaggerated fiction about the horrors that lurked in the Vietnamese night. It is not uncommon for wars to bring about such legends. And it is very common for story tellers to play off these mental pictures when framing their dramas. My grandfather told me stories of massed bayonet charges across no-man's-land during World War I. I grew up with visions of these heroics in the back of my mind. It wasn't until I was a history student in college that I came to realize how little such actions had to do with the massive death toll of the Great War. There are similar misconceptions about the actual dangers of the war in Vietnam. Perhaps some rudimentary knowledge of the weaponry and the logistics in play might clear things up. It seems only logical that once there is an understanding of who had what and how many of them actually were in use, a more realistic picture can be drawn.

The first thing that needs to be understood is that the struggle in Vietnam was an old one, dating back before there was an American presence there. The area had been prone to violence of one type or another, for centuries, but we will look only at the seventy years or so before America entered the fray.

The French moved into the area in the 1880s, claiming it as French Indochina. It was a typical eastern colony of a European nation, held in check by troops and by bribery of local officials. Because of that, nationalistic feelings arose over the decades, and with such emotions comes the propensity for armed insurrection. I am not going to digress into a history lesson here. I am merely setting up the understanding that most of the native combatants were armed with a variety of weapons that were either begged, borrowed, or stolen.

By the time American troops were on the ground in South Vietnam in the early 1960s, the local guerrillas, known as the Viet Cong, were using Chinese communist-supplied AK-47 assault rifles, SKS battle rifles, and various kinds of rocket-propelled grenades (RPGs). These all fall under the "begged" category. Artillery was, for the most part, nonexistent in areas where the VC were the main combatants. They did, from time to time, get their hands on Russian-designed .51-caliber machine guns and some of the larger mortars. This had to come under the heading of "borrowed" equipment because it took trained arms experts to keep them working. The "stolen" equipment was everything the guerrillas could liberate from the American and ARVN troops who weren't paying attention to business. This group of weapons was vast and pretty scary when you consider what awesome firepower the Americans brought to Vietnam. Anything that could be liberated was liberated if it didn't have someone watching it night and day.

Having explained all this, I have left out the weapon that caused a boatload of death, destruction, and mayhem, as well as much of the dread and a great deal of the hype about the Vietnam experience. The nemesis of anyone who ever walked down a trail in the darkness of the Vietnamese night was the booby trap.

Everyone who ever thought about service in Vietnam had a dread of what might be lurking in the dark nights of that war-torn country. The coverage that ambush action got in the press made it seem that Victor Charlie was the master of the night ambush. Actually, that was not the case. When the facts are laid out for examination, they bear out the indisputable fact that the Americans did far worse damage by night ambush than did the communist guerrillas. The Viet Cong were a small, irregular force that had to hide its numbers and move from place to place under cover of darkness. That being the case, they were vulnerable to night ambush attacks. The American forces moved about at will during the day, severely restricting the daylight action of the Viet Cong by the very presence of American firepower in any given area. When night fell, the Americans stopped their units from moving and sent out ambush patrols to hinder the VC, who were limited to moving after sunset. The truth is that the Americans became the masters of the night ambush, along deeply hidden and forgotten trails. That being said, I must admit that the legend of the jungle being filled with faceless killing devices of a sinister, frightening, and diabolical nature was all too true.

The booby trap is, by nature, a handy gadget for combatants who are short on personnel and long on ingenuity. It can be as simple or as complex as the machinery at hand allows and is more powerful as a weapon of dread than as an actual instrument of destruction. The fact that the struggles in Vietnam had lasted for decades made the whole country a depository for booby traps, some of which had been lurking in wait for forty years. This played hob with the fears of everyone who was ever forced to walk into the contested wilderness and ran a few chills up and down the spines of people who only thought about it.

In the early years, when the Viet Minh, or revolutionary guerrillas, were struggling against the French, extremely simple mechanisms of destruction were employed to slow down the enemy. Simple pits were dug knee deep in the soft earth and filled with sharpened bamboo stakes. These were covered with brush or bamboo and were quite a painful surprise when you stepped on them. Heavy logs lined with sharp bamboo spikes were drawn up into the trees by ropes and released by a trip wire, to swing down and deliver devastating blows to the unwary enemy. Such simple devices were still around by the dawn of the 1970s, but they had been joined by a whole new and even more frightening family of explosive devices that were just as clever and a whole lot more devastating.

When talking about booby traps we have to revisit the beg, borrow, and steal, mindset of the enemy. The booby trap is devised to be set and left to hinder the movements of the opposing forces. In such cases, a group like the Viet Cong could not afford to use up their limited resources, so almost all explosive booby traps were made from whatever they could find or steal from the American and ARVN forces. It is sad to admit, but most of the explosive booby traps I personally saw were made from American-issued materials.

Simple is always best. If you can make something that doesn't need any battery power or moving parts, it is less likely to fail when it is engaged. The most elementary of these devices came in the form of a simple hand grenade in a tin can. Over and over again, we came across American hand grenades that had been slipped into tin cans that were secured to tree trunks. The pin was pulled on the grenade and the safety wire removed, and the safety lever, or spoon, was held in place by the sides of the tin can. A trip wire was attached to the grenade and stretched across the trail. When an unsuspecting pedestrian hit the wire, the grenade was jerked from the can, the spoon was released, and three seconds later there was a loud boom. It was a simple and effective device, especially at night. If you hit the wire in the dark, you could hear the thump of the grenade hitting the ground. You knew at that point that you had about three seconds, but you had no idea which way to run. It was often worse for the guy behind you because he had no idea what was going on.

The use of flashlight batteries stepped up the booby-trap technology to a higher level. It takes only three ohms of electricity to set off a blasting cap. That means a simple flashlight battery has more than enough power to set off explosive devices as big as a thousand-pound bomb. This put the VC in a game of larger stakes.

The trigger for electrical booby traps needs to be amazingly simple to work without failure. The interrupted circuit is the most elementary of these devices and can be made from wire and anything that does not conduct electricity. A simple clothespin and a plastic spoon make an excellent trigger.

An explosive, such as C-4, a length of wire, and a blasting cap are needed. A clothespin, a plastic spoon, and a flashlight battery are also necessary. The blasting cap is attached to the detonation wire, then the cap is inserted into the explosives. The detonation wire is stretched and wrapped around one side of the pinchers of the clothespin. The other side of the clothespin pinchers is wrapped with another wire that is connected to the flashlight battery. The plastic spoon is inserted between the two pinchers of the clothespin so the wires do not touch, interrupting the circuit. A trip wire is stretched across the trail with one end secured to a tree and the other tied to the handle of the plastic spoon. When the unsuspecting victim walks through the trip wire, the spoon is jerked from between the two pinchers of the clothes pin, causing the two ends of the wire to touch, closing the circuit and passing electricity to the blasting cap. This, of course, causes a huge explosion. It's simple, easy to set up, and can be rigged to detonate any size explosive charge. The best part, or worst part, depending on whether you or the enemy is setting up this little surprise, is that all this can be done using things snatched from the enemy.

The thought of tripping such a device while moving quietly through the wooded landscape was always on the mind of the combat soldier in Vietnam. The actual damage done by land mines and booby traps was considerable, as I would discover personally during the invasion into Cambodia. The most strident reminder that the Viet Cong were the masters of such automatic warfare came to us in February 1970.

The company had been working on the edges of the Michelin rubber plantation for a week or so. We were circled up in a clear area on the eastern side of the rubber trees, doing some routine chores for Uncle Sam. It was the day that men from the Finance Corps came out to exchange our military payment certificates. American personnel were not allowed to carry US currency in a combat zone, so the government paid us in military payment certificates. These were little paper bills that looked not unlike Monopoly money. To keep the black market on the run, the army picked a day, every now and again, and sent out agents to exchange the old bills for new ones. The new bills had different pictures on them and rendered the old ones useless. They were only good for lighting cigarettes after the exchange date.

On this day, we were all lined up in front of a card table that sat under the shade of a stretched-out tarp. Two Finance Corps officers were counting out the new payment certificates and collecting the old ones when a huge explosion in the distance shook the ground under our feet, causing the two finance guys to duck to the ground and look absolutely panic-stricken. The rest of us flinched a little and then looked at each other. We knew the blast had come from a good ways off, but the jolt under our feet had told us that this had been a big one. Pretty soon the radios began to sing with confused chatter, and a picture of what had happened began to evolve.

As it turned out, two tracks from the reconnaissance platoon were on their way into the base camp of Dau Tieng when the lead track tripped a booby trap made of an unexploded five-hundred-pound bomb. The explosion was so fierce that it all but vaporized the lead track and seven men who were aboard. The medics and graves registration people had to match up body parts to figure out how many people had been killed. It was the largest and most devastating booby-trap experience any of us could remember. The incident became legendary within the battalion and was a perfect example of the industrious nature of the Vietnamese people. They had dug up a five-hundred-pound US Air Force bomb from the place where it had landed and failed to go off. They carried this heavy device through the forests, at night, daring discovery by American ambush patrols, until they reached the place they wanted to bury it. They had to dig a hole under the road large enough to hide this thing and then camouflage the dig site so it would not be discovered. Exercising great patience, they waited until Americans were working in that area once again before they hooked it up.

This incident left an indelible impression on everybody who ever heard of it, and most certainly on those of us who actually heard the explosion that morning. From that day forward, the members of C Company carried with them a sort of fatalistic attitude about our chances against the booby traps and mines of the Viet Cong.

Track Fifteen

CUE: *Folsom Prison Blues*, JOHNNY CASH

Every man who has ever stood in the line of battle has had to come to the realization that death is a part of that endeavor. Each soldier finds his own way into and out of the mindset that must accompany combat, and each must deal with it in his own way. Most make that difficult journey in the company of their comrades and come out of it emotionally scarred but a bit wiser in the realities of life at a more elemental level. Some wait until civilian life has resumed in a more peaceful place to deal with the emotional impact. Some never deal with it at all. I suppose there has never been a war that has not left some of its emotionally shattered veterans standing hollow-eyed on street corners, still traumatized by the human price such wars always exact. Certainly the war in Vietnam was no exception.

I have often thought about those war-shattered personalities that have never been able to shake off the emotional effects of a year in the fray, so many decades ago. It is a subject that has haunted me and made me search my own soul and my own experience for an answer. Why did I and so many like me manage to come home and reenter society without being socially and emotionally crippled by regret of actions taken in combat? After years of reflection on the subject, I think I may have stumbled on an answer. I don't know why I never thought about it before now.

As a boy who was raised in the ranch country of west Texas, I was schooled in the art of shooting from the earliest age. The men of my family were all great hunters, and my father was one of the greatest wing shots in America. He was chosen as a member of the US Marine Corps Skeet Team, which gives some credence to my brags about his prowess with a gun. Safety was always a big thing with my father, and so when it was my time to begin shooting, he introduced me to the power of the gun in an unforgettable way.

On a cool autumn morning, we walked out to the open pit my family used as a shooting backdrop. My father carried his shotgun under his arm, and I was excited at the prospect of beginning my lessons on shooting. As we neared the far end of the shooting pit, I saw that there was a small wire cage there. Inside was a full-grown hen, white and quite pretty, with a red comb that seemed to flip this way and that as she cocked her head to see what we were doing. As we approached, my father slipped the gun from under his arm and jacked a shell into the chamber. His hand came to my shoulder, and steadily he brought me up to stand next to him, facing the cage and the chicken inside. He bent low and said to me, in a soft but serious voice, "I want you to remember this. Never point a gun at anybody." He then stood erect, placed the shotgun to his shoulder and fired, point blank, at the helpless chicken in the cage. Instantly the living thing was turned into a bloody, palpitating mess before my young eyes.

I never forgot that moment or the lesson it imparted. From the first time a firearm was placed in my hands, there was never a doubt in my mind what devastating things it could do to a living body. The scene came back to me again and again as a young man, but never as strongly as it did on the first night I stood over the limp form of a human being who had died by my hands. Other nights would follow, until the remembrance of my father's words faded. They slipped away to be replaced by a sort of apathy. It was a feeling that seemed to come from the fatigue of the long, dark nights and the determination that I would get back home, no matter what it took. As time went by, I began to recognize the same look in the eyes of those with whom I shared those dark nights. There was recognition between us that was a sort of wordless understanding, never spoken, only seen in the lackluster stare that was the hallmark of those who had met combat head on. Somehow the faces of the dead seemed to fade away until they all seemed to have only one face. Oddly enough, everyone agreed that it was the face of the first one.

If these are the thoughts that haunt those who seem never to have gotten over the Vietnam experience, then there must be a reason. There has to be a reason why some transcend their military horrors and move on, and others do not. I believe the secret lies in choices made during that tumultuous time. The choices made could actually be the key to self-salvation. I am fairly certain this was true in my case.

Sometime in March, or maybe it was April, we were on our way to an ambush position in an area known as War Zone C. We had been out for many nights and were all bordering on the edge of exhaustion. As usual, we moved out on a circuitous route and hid in the underbrush, waiting for the dark to cover us. As we lay there in the shade of the trees, several of the guys were silently playing cards. I had never been particularly lucky at the poker table, so I took out a paperback book and began to read.

After an hour or so, I put down the book and began to stretch. It was then I caught sight of a movement in the tree line about a hundred yards to our left. I froze and watched carefully, until I could see the full form of a man as he walked out of the trees and stopped, facing away from our group's position. I held my breath as I watched him lay his rifle against a tree and begin to urinate, completely unaware I was watching him. My eyes swept the tree line until I was sure he was alone, then I reached across the prone and napping figure of Dennis Kinney, picked up his M-16 rifle, and softly brought it up to my shoulder. I still carried the tommy gun, which was not made for single shots at so great a distance. Kinney's rifle was the weapon I needed. I held my breath and drew a bead, square in the middle of the back of the unsuspecting VC. It was an easy shot for me, and I knew it would drop him without a second shot being fired. I held my breath and placed my finger on the trigger, waiting until I was sure he was perfectly still. I waited a second longer and then found myself smiling. I held my fire and said to myself, "Not today, Victor Charlie." I took the rifle from my shoulder and watched as the unsuspecting enemy finished his biological function, picked up his rifle, and disappeared into the woods. I let him go.

I never told any of the guys about this encounter. I didn't think about it again for many years. When I did, I came to realize that this one action might be the very reason I was saved some of the anguish so many experienced after the war. When I had time to think about it, it seemed to me I had been given a choice that day. I was like so many others who had been given no choice at all in where we would go or what we would do in Vietnam. It was not our choice that sent us into harm's way or placed us in those moments that haunted the memories of so many. We simply had no choice in the matter. But on this day I was given a clear choice. I was given a moment in which it was my choice alone whether a man would live or die, and in that singular moment, I chose to let him go. In that fleeting instant, I discovered that I was still a feeling human being.

Such a moment never came again. At least, I never made the same decision again. But somewhere, if he lived through the war, there is a man who has no idea that I held his life in my hands and chose to let him keep it. What is even more bizarre is the possibility that this same man, by the act of being in such a position, may have saved me from the recurring horrors that so many returned from the war to face. He gave me the chance to see whether I was still a decent human being. He gave me the chance to make a decision for life in a place where life had become cheap, and I sense that I owe him something for that.

I will always think that most of us had some similar moment in our war experience. I tend to believe that those who returned with an incurable cancer on their soul may have faced such a moment and made a decision that haunts them to this very day.

Track Sixteen

CUE: *I Started a Joke*, THE BEE GEES

I suppose in every profession there is a certain mindset that outsiders simply don't understand. So it is with every generation of combat infantrymen. No matter what the war, there grows a sense of humor that is singular to the combat soldier and completely misunderstood by the rest of the army in particular, and the world in general. It comes with the territory, like the suntan from endless days under the blaze of the Asian sky and the thousand-yard stare from endless nights in the darkness. Things that would not have seemed funny in a world filled with more sanity took on a sarcastic humor that bordered on absolute cruelty when viewed through the prism of death and destruction. The infantry sense of humor was dark by necessity for it was a release from daily pressures that had to escape or cause permanent damage to the emotional stability of the combatants. We were trapped for a year in a world without mercy or forgiveness, and so we learned to laugh. We laughed at strange things, but we laughed. At times this dark mirth may have been our salvation.

Pain and suffering was our business, so it was often those very things that triggered our outrageous sense of humor. Even pain inflicted on our own numbers sometimes became the object of laughter. It was simply a matter of how it happened and what was going on at the time.

We had been sent to the edge of the Renegade Woods to guard a company of combat engineers who were cutting down the forest. It was kind of a vacation. We were out of the area where most of the preinvasion stuff was going on before the Cambodian incursion. All we had to do was watch to see that the engineers didn't get shot, and drink sodas. It was really easy duty.

One afternoon, Thomas "Lurch" Glubka took the Two Four track into the laager site to pick up the mail. He was by himself because he was only going about five hundred yards from us. This gave Lurch the chance to hot rod his track a bit. If Lurch was anything, he was a frustrated drag racer. On this very hot day, Lurch ran at top speed for the circle of tracks and shot over the berm of earth that surrounded them. This caused a huge dust cloud and a lot of complaints from those who were close by. As he pulled up to the place where the Chinook helicopter was discharging its cargo, he was greeted with good-natured jeers, a mailbag for the 2nd Platoon, and a brand new replacement who was on his first trip out into the bush. The first sergeant brought the boy to the Two Four track and assigned him to the 2nd Platoon. Lurch opened the top hatch on the APC and threw the mailbag down inside. He told the new guy to get onboard and went off to trade for some C rations with fruit in them.

By the time Lurch got back, the new guy was sitting on top of the track, behind the gunner's hatch. Lurch realized that the boy was not in a very stable position and decided to shake him up a bit on his first track ride. Lurch climbed into the driver's seat, turned up the volume on the old red radio that was tied on the gunner's hatch, and goosed the engine. The Two Four track spun around in the loose dirt and raced for the earthen berm. As the APC shot over the mound of earth and became airborne, Lurch must have been in hot rodder's heaven. He was in his element, and the new guy was scrambling and looking for something to hold onto. What he found was the edge of the cargo hatch on top of the track, which Lurch had forgotten to fasten after tossing the mail into the belly of the beast. When the Two Four track became airborne, the hatch came open and raised up under the knees of the new arrival. The kid grabbed onto the edge of the rising hatch, the track hit the ground with a huge impact, and the hatch slammed shut with the new kid's fingers wrapped around it.

It must have really hurt. The kid must have yelled like crazy, but with the engine revving at full speed, the radio blasting in his ears, and Lurch singing at the top of his lungs, no one knew the kid was trapped like that until Lurch brought the track to a halt and turned to introduce the new guy to us all.

Of course, all his fingers were broken. In fact, we all wondered how he managed not to lose a finger or two in the process. It took four strong men and an ax handle to get the hatch open and free the ashen-faced new guy. The medics came out and immediately took him back to the laager site. He was flown back to the rear on the same Chinook helicopter on which he had come out. We all marveled at this. Here was the perfect tour in Vietnam. A guy comes out for his first day in a combat unit, breaks his fingers, earns a Purple Heart, and goes back in on the same helicopter in which he had arrived. He spends twenty minutes in the line and gets to go home a decorated veteran. We laughed about this for months. I suspect there was a bit of envy in each chuckle.

Some of the humor took the form of running jokes that went on for months. It was so in the case of Larry McCoster, who managed to shoot himself in the head with his own machine gun. It was a lucky quirk of fate that McCoster was not killed in this odd incident.

We were stopped on the edge of a small patch of woods north of the base camp of Cu Chi. There had been some trouble with one of the M-60 machine guns jamming, so several shade-tree gunsmiths had collaborated to get the thing working again. When McCoster tried test firing the gun, a one-in-a-million freak occurrence happened. One of the rounds fired from the gun hit something in the tree line and came straight back at the gunner. The bullet tore a hole in his right ear and glanced off the mastoid bone, doing no real damage but knocking McCoster cold.

Everyone ran to see what had happened. We were all relieved when the medics told us the wound was not serious and all McCoster would suffer from was a few hours of disorientation and a pretty weird-looking hole in his ear. The beauty of it all was that he would get to spend a day or two in the evac hospital. He would stay there until he knew his name and was clearheaded enough to return to combat duty. That is where the joke comes in. Poor Larry McCoster remained out to lunch for close to a week. The medics told us that the doctors in the rear were thinking seriously of sending him back to the States for observation. He was going to get out of the line and go home. It was at this point that Larry McCoster opened his mouth and said the worst thing he could possibly say.

"Oh. Now I remember!"

Needless to say, they sent him back to us. He lost the perfect chance to get out of the field and go back to the world by simply failing to keep his mouth shut.

As the months went by, the McCoster saga became the source of many a laugh on a long dark night. When things seemed particularly bad or when we were all disgusted and exhausted, someone would pipe up and say, "Oh. Now I remember!" and the night would become filled with smothered laughter. If McCoster was within earshot on such nights, the muffled giggles were usually followed by the standard retort, "F— you!"

Not all the twisted humor was reserved for American mishaps. The Viet Cong provided us with moments of cruel humor as well. The fact that they spent most of their time trying to do us bodily harm made it that much easier to see them as the objects of sadistic humor.

During a rainy night ambush, somewhere near Xuan Loc, we began to hear a strange sound coming from the wet darkness of the forest. It was an odd sound that none of us could identify. We thought the sounds of the falling rain might be distorting the noise, but still we could not make any kind of identification, so we all stayed awake and on alert status the whole night. Hours passed and the noise became more and more intermittent, but it seemed louder with each passing hour. We waited for dawn with trepidation. There was no telling what new device of the enemy awaited us, and we were understandably nervous about it.

When the sun came up and painted gray light across the forest floor, we spread out in a line and began to move through the woods in the direction of the menacing sound. Each man was alert and ready to fire on any threat that might present itself. None of us were ready for what we actually found.

During the night, there had been the sounds of mortar rounds bursting to the west of us. This was not unusual, and because we had been advised by radio that it was an American fire mission, we attached no importance to it. But it was of paramount importance to one of the local enemy soldiers.

As we began to close in on the stark sound, it began to change pitch and come to us in shorter spurts of scratchy noises. It began to sound somewhat familiar to me, but I was too nervous and alert for any danger to concentrate on it. Then we rounded a small group of trees and there it was. At first we stood at the ready, looking about for any sign of danger, and then, slowly, we were overcome with relief marked by ragged waves of laughter.

Seated on the ground and leaning back against a tree was the body of a Viet Cong soldier. There was a bleeding wound in his head from which protruded the ragged edge of a piece of mortar shrapnel. He had evidently been hit by the mortar attack of the previous night and made it this far before he gave up the ghost. It was not his grisly death that provoked our laughter but the fact that he was sitting there with a live duck under his arm. The poor bird was locked in the grip of the dead man, held fast against the trunk of the tree and unable to work himself free. He had evidently been trapped like that for most of the night, and it was his frustrated quacking we had heard through the rain-soaked darkness. It was simply too ironic for words, so we laughed, freed the duck, and made our way back to the tracks. We would never again give much credence to the thought of new and strange-sounding weapons.

The vein of hard humor ran deep and seemed to give us a peculiar sense of the ironic that many who were outside the brotherhood of combat could not seem to comprehend. Often, what seemed funny in one instance became chilling and deadly serious in another. The difference between them was a matter of what was happening at the time and how close the situation was to your own mindset. I can think of two incidents that stand out as examples.

On one moonlit night, our ambush patrol was set up on the edge of an active rice field. About midnight, two enemy soldiers came walking along the rice dikes. They were talking and simply strolling along together, no threat to anyone but themselves, when the older of the two suddenly stopped. He was unaware that nine men were staring at him with their fingers on the triggers of their weapons. He began pointing at one of our Claymore mines, which was badly hidden and showed up in the bright moonlight. The soldier handed his rifle to his colleague and reached down to pluck the Claymore from its hiding place. We all stopped breathing, frozen in anticipation of what was to come, while the two Vietnamese stood calmly talking in the moonlight, the older one holding the active mine in his hands. It was like watching a foreign movie without subtitles. We could not understand a word the older man was saying, but it was perfectly clear what he meant. He was telling his younger partner how careless and foolish the Americans were to leave such good stuff lying around all over the place. He began walking toward us, happily winding the detonation wire around the body of the live mine. We bit our lips and ducked low behind the rice dike while one of our number squeezed the clacker and spread the enemy soldier all over the rice field. It was grim, but it was a lot like watching a macabre Buster Keaton silent movie. On another night, a similar situation produced markedly different reactions, at least for me.

It had been a long night, one of many in the unending string of ambush patrols for the 2nd Platoon. It was dark of the moon, and consequently the night was inky, making every sound and breeze a source of nervous anticipation. In the early morning hours, probably about 3:00 a.m. or so, a dark, undulating line of shadows came into our view. It became evident that it was a group of Vietnamese creeping through the darkness, running parallel to our position. As they drew near to us, we realized they were going to pass between us and the Claymore mines that were stretched out in front of us for about twenty-five yards or so. Those who were awake and on guard held their breath as the shadowy figures moved along, only yards away. Suddenly the whole line came to a halt. The dark figure leading the group had stopped and was bending over. He had tangled himself up in one of the detonation wires that led to the Claymores. He swore silently under his breath and yanked at the stubborn wire, then froze in his tracks. He stayed that way for a moment or two, then slowly turned his head in our direction. He knew what he had in his hand. He knew it was attached to a Claymore mine, and he knew one of us was on the other end. In that dark moment in time, he knew he was going to die.

I have thought of this man many times in the years since I left the war zone. I have pictured him and tried to imagine what he must have felt at that moment. Although the situation was not unlike some of the others that had provoked mirth, I have never been able to feel anything but sympathy for him in those last moments of his life. I suppose it's like the standard explanation given when a joke bombs at a party.

"I guess you had to be there."

Track Seventeen

CUE: *Fire and Rain*, JAMES TAYLOR

"Somebody help me!"

The fear in the voice had a ragged edge that cut into my soul and touched a place deep inside me where the worst of the worst fears reside. We had all heard the shots. The AK–47 has a distinctive signature sound and loudly announced that the shots, which split the silence and shadowy gloom of the forest, had come from the VC.

The voice came from Olsen. I couldn't see him. He was hidden from view by the thick underbrush, but the desperation that vibrated from his cry for help sank deep into me. It was the last sound he would ever make. I never saw him again. We were engaged in a crawling and shooting firefight that moved beyond the place where Olsen was hit. The medics came to his aide, and the dustoff choppers carried him away, but those of us in the 2nd Platoon simply had to act as if he had never been there. As far as I can recall, his name remained unmentioned among us for possibly thirty years. It was much that way with all who paid the ultimate price. They were suddenly gone, and for us to dwell on the fact could become disabling, so the dead were quietly erased from everyday thought and conversation. Their memory was laid aside, in my own case for decades, until another war claimed young men in battle. Funerals were held, and the sounds of guns fired in salute and bugles brought out the emotions that had been swept under the rug of my psyche. I found myself flinching at the stark crack of the rifles and felt my tears flowing for those who had left us one by one so many years ago without so much as a "Goodbye." I am certain it is the same for all of us who remain.

I suppose the death of Joe Raber was the only exception to this exclusion standard, but Raber's death was an exception in so many ways that it deserves a chapter of its own.

I imagine this silent treatment regarding the dead is an age-old custom among those who must go again and again into harm's way. Among the troops that took the battle to the enemy in Vietnam, there was a temporary nature to all situations. The tour of duty was only a year, and the combat company was constantly involved with troops who were leaving as experienced veterans or arriving as raw replacements. During this revolving evolution, there was one constant hope. If a man made good and lived through his whole time with a combat company, he would eventually gain the much-coveted title of "short timer."

Those who had less than thirty days left in-country were treated with a certain amount of deference. They were often excused from risky ambush patrols and were occasionally assigned to off-line jobs, some of which were back in the base camps. In this subtle way, faces that had been a part of the daily life of the platoon simply slipped away and were replaced by new ones. Being "short" was something every line trooper hoped for, but to become a short timer you had to be lucky enough to make the whole tour without getting so bunged up that you were sent to the hospital or assigned to another platoon. For this reason, each man desperately held onto his place on the track, often passing up better assignments where he might never have the chance of experiencing the coveted treatment of the short timer.

The tracks were circled up on a small hilltop, and we were taking some time to eat and write letters before saddling up to go out on yet another ambush patrol. I had reached the point of being one of the more senior members on the Two Zero track. Charlie Dunn had rotated back to the States, and Greg Balsley, who was the driver, was soon to leave for home as well. I was eyeing the position of driver because it would mean I would get to stay with the track and never go out on ambush patrol again. Perc McCaa was also interested in the driver's job. He was much better qualified than I was because of his experience back home with heavy farm equipment. The whole question became settled in a strange way that still bothers me a little.

Several of us were sitting on the ground when we were approached by a tall platoon sergeant who had the unfortunate nickname "Shaky Jake." He came up, towering over us from his six-foot-two height, and announced,

"Stoney, pack your stuff and get on the chopper. You're going to sharpshooter's school."

I was stunned. This tall, lanky noncom was indicating I had been chosen to go back to the Cu Chi base camp to be trained as a sniper. This was not a good thing for a man who had been out on enough ambush patrols that he was looking to get out of such fun and games in the dark. Snipers spent almost every night out in the bush, looking for someone to shoot. To say that I rebelled at the suggestion is an understatement.

Looking back on the moment, I probably was a bit over the top in my refusal. I am certain I was chosen because of my unearned reputation as the last of the frontiersmen who could follow trails and find his way through the wilderness like Daniel Boone or Davy Crockett. No matter what the reason, my refusal became quite loud and prompted Shaky Jake's rebuttal to attain even greater volume. Naturally, the argument began to draw a crowd. Getting the attention of bystanders was not so bad, but when 1st Sergeant Strain showed up, one look at his face told me something was about to happen. This man had been through World War II, the Korean War and Vietnam, all in the infantry. He had no sense of humor and very little patience with what the army now sent him as soldiers.

In soft and gruff tones, he asked Shaky Jake what was going on. The answer was pretty accurate but delivered in a high, excited voice that obviously irritated the ranking sergeant, or "top kick." He looked at me for a long moment, then turned to Larry Grubbs, who was still seated on the ground. He ordered Grubbs to pack up and take the chopper to sharpshooter's School. Slowly, he turned and gestured for me to follow him. I walked behind him without saying a word, wondering with every step what kind of just desserts awaited me. We came to a stop next to the command track, the company commander's track. The first sergeant reached up on top of the track and pulled down the headset that was plugged into the command radio. "Here you go," he growled in his quiet, authoritative voice. "Try using your big mouth on this."

In this way, with no more ceremony than that, I was no longer a member of the 2nd Platoon nor a member of the family on the Two Zero track. I was the machine gunner and radioman on the command track. I had become one of those who were there one moment and gone the next. My military life would change in almost every way, some good and some bad. My close family ties to the 2nd Platoon would fade as they continued to go out on ambush and lose members of the group to enemy fire, and yet, I had achieved one of my goals. I was no longer a line troop. I was off ambush and part of the command group, which should have made me more protected. Oddly enough, it would almost cost me my life.

"They come and they go," 1st Sergeant Strain used to say. "They come and they go. They all have the same face, and that face is very young."

I'm sure he borrowed the quote from someone else, but it was true from his experienced point of view. It was true, and I had made the first step on that journey of change. I was no longer a member of the 2nd Platoon.

Track Eighteen

CUE: *The Weight*, THE BAND

Life as a member of the command unit was completely different and wholly unexpected. There was no time to acclimate to the differences. We were on the move as soon as I threw my stuff into the back of the track. I was now the gunner, which meant I was riding in the gunner's hatch. This was, without a doubt, the best position to be in. I was seated behind a .50-caliber Browning machine gun and surrounded by a thick steel shield that could deflect anything but an artillery round. I wore a headset that was plugged into battalion and company channels and could hear pretty much everything that was going on around us. This was a step up and away from being a simple rifleman who crawled around in the bushes much of the time.

The rest of the command unit was made up of men who were trained for just such work. Carnes, the driver, was the only track jockey I ever met who had actually been to APC school. He knew the track inside and out and was highly respected for his mechanical expertise. He even knew the .50-caliber gun better than I did. I suspect he looked on me with a great deal of disdain, since I had been pulled from the line to sit next to him. I have to say that his opinion of me was, for the most part, pretty accurate.

There were two trained radio operators. The track not only had battalion and company radios but also boasted a "secure set" that could send and receive scrambled messages that supposedly could not be understood by listening ears on the same frequency. This piece of technology was testy and needed trained hands. The radio telephone operators, or RTOs, were responsible for keeping the company commander in contact with everyone at all times. When he left the track, one or sometimes both of the RTOs followed him with radios strapped to their backs. Both of these communications zealots were specially trained for the job, and oddly enough, both of them had amazingly blond hair. In fact, their hair was so light it was easy to spot them at a distance. It is not surprising that one of them went by the nickname "Cotton." I confess that I cannot remember the name of the other. I do seem to recall that it had a sort of Scandinavian ring to it, which might explain the pale blond hair.

Off and on, the command track carried an officer from the artillery along with his radioman. Because he was the forward observer for the big guns in the rear, the officer was always referred to as "Fo," thereby losing his personal identity and real name. That seems to be an age-old military problem.

Members of Company C, 1/5 Infantry (Mechanized), February 1970. Clockwise from bottom center: Larry Vunak, Palo Zavala, Doc Tap (medic), Joe Raber, Lester Lorig, Oscar Solis, Tom "Lurch" Glubka. (*Larry Vunak*)

Leaving Fire Support Base Devin. (*Robert Sweatmon*)

A member of Company C: Dennis Kinney. An M113 armored personnel carrier is in the background. Mechanized infantry rode these "tracks" into battle. (*Robert Sweatmon*)

Company C destroying a suspected Viet Cong site near the Ho Bo Woods. (*Robert Sweatmon*)

A member of Company C: Charlie Dunn, Sioux Indian, squad leader on the two zero track. (*Robert Sweatmon*).

A member of Company C: Larry Vunak. (*Robert Sweatmon*)

A member of Company C: Hal Greer playing with Vietnamese orphans. Hal was killed in action. (*Robert Sweatmon*)

A member of Company C: the author Robert "Stoney" Sweatmon on radio watch in the communications bunker at Tay Ninh. (*Robert Sweatmon*)

The author's ambush patrol gear. Because the Viet Cong moved mostly at night, members of the company were ordered to establish ambush sites each night in order to encounter Viet Cong forces. (*Robert Sweatmon*)

A member of Company C: Raymond "Tex" White. This was the last photograph taken of him. (*Robert Sweatmon*)

A member of Company C: "Doc" Glover, the medic. (*Robert Sweatmon*)

A member of Company C: Oscar Solis. His foot is bandaged from a grenade fragment that hit him during an ambush patrol. Oscar lost his life during the invasion of Cambodia. (*Robert Sweatmon*)

Cu Chi market from two zero track on the move. (*Robert Sweatmon*)

A member of Company C: Steve (C. L.) Clements, the second platoon sergeant and respected philosopher. (*Mark Coleman*)

The two four track, named "Born Loser," with Joe Raber, Phil Harding, and Lurch Glubka aboard. (*Mark Coleman*)

A member of Company C: Lester Lorig. Les was the author's ambush partner on many long, dark nights. (*Lester Loring*)

A member of Company C: Captain Mitchell Meilstrup, commanding officer. (*Robert Sweatmon*)

Members of Company C: Soldiers prepared for ambush patrol. (*George Bradley*)

A member of Company C: George Bradley, driver of the two four track.
(*George Bradley*)

Members of Company C: Gil Gilreath and Verle Bagley in their ambush gear.
(*Gil Gilreath*)

A flame track. (*Robert Sweatmon*)

Members of Company C: Joe Raber and Greg Balsley. (*Mark Coleman*)

Checking a village. (*Robert Sweatmon*)

Searching for Viet Cong tunnels in Ho Bo Woods. (*Robert Sweatmon*)

Tracks moving out after the rainy season. (*Gil Gilreath*)

Burning VC bunkers. (*Robert Sweatmon*)

Track in grass. (*Larry Vunak*)

A .50 caliber machine gun. (*Larry Vunak*)

Nui Ba Den Mountain from Tay Ninh Base Camp. (*Robert Sweatmon*)

The shadow of Nui Ba Den Mountain. (*Robert Sweatmon*)

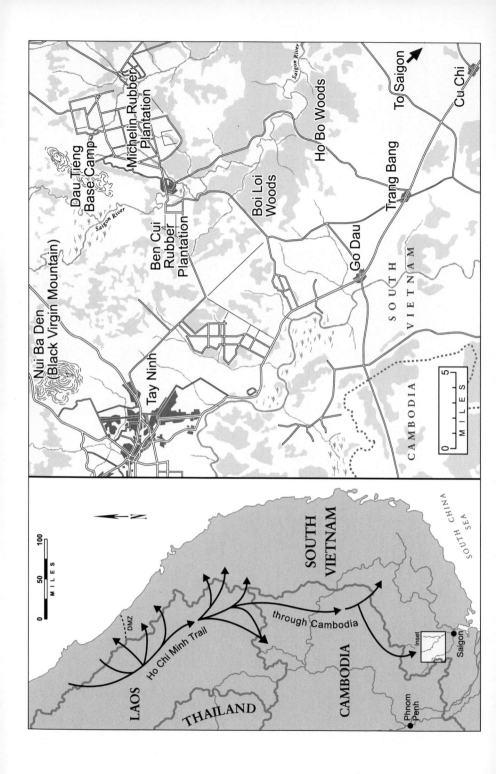

The company commander was Captain Mitchell Meilstrup. He was an impressive man in many ways, but his eyes told the real story. He wore glasses, and the sparks that flew from his eyes in moments of conflict were unmistakable indicators of a warrior's soul behind the lenses. He was tall and lithe and had a reputation as a seasoned combat commander. In the center of his chest he bore a huge scar that had been gained leading men in combat as a second lieutenant. He was a leader tested by fire, and his very presence seemed to mold the company in his image. The formidable reputation of C Company had come about, in part, because Mitch Meilstrup was its leader. We had been commanded by others, but they could not hold a candle to this man.

As I sat atop my perch on that first day, I could not have felt more out of place. In my heart, I was now an orphan from the Two Zero track and the 2nd Platoon, yet I was in a position envied by some. As we took our place in the line of moving APCs, I set the tommy gun down in the gunner's hatch beside me. I no longer needed it. I had a huge .50-caliber machine gun right in front of me, yet it seemed comforting to have something of the old life within my grasp. It would stay there until the track itself was blown away.

My new duties would be more detail oriented, and I soon found that each move not only could affect my own welfare but also that of so many others. Communications were relayed to and from the company commander through the RTOs when Meilstrup was on the ground, but through the track radio when he was onboard. This meant that much of the time, command decisions and even orders were relayed through me. I became a sort of combat commander's answering service.

Even though I had carried the radio some of the time on ambush patrols, this was altogether different. I now had to deal with everything from resupply communication to calling for dustoff choppers and even relaying attack orders. It was a huge adjustment.

To be truthful, I cannot remember much about my first day in this new position. I am fairly certain I spent those hours stumbling through the new duties and trying to learn as fast as possible. The end of that day, however, sticks in my memory.

At four thirty, Captain Meilstrup leaned over and told me to order the company to circle up. I pressed the button and spoke into the microphone, and the whole company went into action. The tracks began to form their customary defensive circle, and like an army of ants, the troops began digging fighting positions and putting up RPG screens and barbed wire. The enlisted members of the command track complement began to do the same thing, but in our case there was a difference. The platoon tracks formed a huge circle, making a defensive perimeter, but the command track, the medic's track, and the mortar tracks were in the center of that circle. As I looked around me, I realized that in case of attack, I could not shoot in any direction. We were surrounded by our troops. When such attacks did come, it was unnerving to sit and do nothing while the men around the perimeter did all the fighting.

As the first afternoon began to draw to a close, I crawled on top of the track to secure the radio headset out of the weather for the night. I remember looking in the direction of the 2nd Platoon tracks, where I caught sight of a line of men threading their way through the barbed wire and out to an ambush position. I had been with them countless times on such missions. Now I was watching them go. As if he felt my eyes on him, one of the departing figures turned and looked back at me and waved. It was Oscar Solis. In less than a month, he would be dead.

Track Nineteen

CUE: *Take It Easy*, THE EAGLES

"Five Four Whiskey, . . . Five Four Whiskey, . . . Niner Four Oscar."

The scratchy voice in the headset was calling us. It was the voice of battalion command, identified by an ever-changing numerical signature that I had to keep up with. It was a part of the price one paid to step back from the line of battle. I hit the transmission switch and spoke into the microphone.

"Five Four Whiskey, . . . go."

The faceless voice began a litany of lengthy messages about resupply and other mundane details having to do with the daily life of the company. The messages came often and were important, yet I now remember very few of them. Only the voices remain in my memory. I still wonder how the men on the other end of such transmissions managed to pick my words out from the roar of the track motors.

On this afternoon, we were moving along a dirt road in the direction of a village that had been the site of some recent Viet Cong activity. We stopped along the road for Captain Meilstrup to confer with his platoon commanders and to call in resupply for the coming night. While we were stopped, the 2nd Platoon sent out a number of men as pickets on the flank so we would not be sitting ducks for an enemy patrol.

I could hear voices calling from the cover of the underbrush just to our left, and soon the radio crackled in my ear, asking for Lieutenant Phillips. I handed my headset down to him, and Phillips spoke a few terse words into the radio. He handed the headset back up to me and returned to the circle of officers who were gathered in front of the command track. The words they exchanged provoked action. The whole group walked off into the bushes, and before long the radio buzzed in my ear once again with an odd request.

"Stoney, come out here."

To ask a gunner to leave the track was an unusual request, but it was Meilstrup's voice, so I picked up the tommy gun and climbed down. As I started off in the direction the others had taken, the thought occurred to me that I was once again a soldier on the ground, making my way through the bushes. Things hadn't changed so much after all.

As I drew close to the group of officers and picket troops, they were all looking at something on the ground. When I was close enough, I could see that the object of their attention was a fresh pile of human waste. Someone had been at this spot, relieving himself pretty recently. Our Vietnamese scout, a former Viet Cong who had surrendered and then volunteered his services to the Americans, was pointing at the ground and babbling in broken English to anyone who would listen. Meilstrup looked up and motioned for me to come closer. He pushed his glasses back up on his nose, which was a habit that I came to understand as a sign of irritation. His voice was flat and command-like, without emotion, as he spoke to me.

"Phillips here says you're a tracker."

I looked over at Phillips and suddenly realized that my bogus reputation as the last of the frontiersmen was about to fall apart. Phillips pointed down at the pile of human excrement and then to a slight impression in the grass next to it.

"What do you think, cowboy?"

Captain Meilstrup could not hide the tinge of challenge in his voice as I stepped over to look at the still-soft pile of poop.

My heart eased a little when I noticed that there was a clear trail in the grass that led up to the spot in question and then away in the direction parallel to the path of our tracks. Even a novice hunter knows that men make tracks in the grass pushing the stems down in the direction they are walking. I knew at once that whoever this was, he had moved off in the same direction we were going.

"How many?"

Meilstrup's question was short and to the point. I told him these tracks were made by one individual.

"You mean this guy is all by himself?"

The question was as much a test as a query. The intense gaze coming from behind the captain's lenses bore testimony to that. I stammered my answer.

"These tracks were made by only one. There is no telling how many more might be waiting down there where he's heading."

I pointed in the direction the trail led, and suddenly the scout erupted in a loud babble of broken English accompanied by wild gesturing in the opposite direction from that which I had indicated. Meilstrup looked at me and then at Phillips with a withering glance. His words were cold and yet blistering at the same time.

"It seems our scout disagrees. He says they were moving that way. You can go back to the track, Stoney."

As I turned and started making my way through the underbrush, I could hear Phillips's voice stammering a protest and Meilstrup's cutting him off in short order.

"This man is a trained scout who has lived here all his life. I think I'll take his word over some Texas brushpopper."

When we were saddled up and moving again, I expected the captain to be aggravated with me, but he didn't indicate that at all. It had simply been one of the many command decisions of the day, and he was satisfied, at least for the moment. As it turned out, we did not move more than a few hundred yards down that trail when the VC opened a close ambush attack on us. They were exactly where I had indicated they were going.

The fighting was fierce. Rocket-propelled grenades came from the underbrush, and the crack of AK-47s could be heard all around us. The line troops bailed off and maneuvered toward the enemy. The tracks turned and supported the ground troops with .50-caliber machine-gun fire. As quickly as it had begun, it ended. We had no bodies to show for the engagement except our own. Hal Greer from the Two Zero track was wounded seriously and died after he was dusted off.

When we had moved on and circled up for the night, Captain Meilstrup asked me to find the scout. Though I looked for him, he was nowhere to be found. We never saw him again. He simply disappeared into the Vietnamese countryside. We never discovered whether he was simply mistaken in his determination of which way the enemy was moving or setting us up for an attack. From that day forward, I cannot remember the captain ever asking for or listening to an opinion from one of the Vietnamese scouts. He did, from time to time, casually ask me what I thought about such things. I think he suspected that my frontier reputation was a bit exaggerated, but he asked just the same.

The incident along the trail that cost us Hal Greer was never mentioned again. When we received word by radio that Greer had bought the farm, the first sergeant asked me to go over and give the news to the 2nd Platoon. It was uncomfortable. They took the news as always, with quiet resignation, and then offered me a cold soda from the ice chest on the Two Zero track. There was a noticeable difference in their interaction with me that night. They were friendly, and we were still comrades who had shared much, but it was obvious I was no longer a member of that close family. I had taken a step away from them, and already the ranks had closed behind me. As I walked back to the command track, I felt a tinge of loneliness that I have found hard to put into words until this moment. A chapter of my life had drawn to a close.

Track Twenty

CUE: *Stuck in the Middle with You*, STEALERS WHEEL

The absolute absurdity of war is often lost on all but the participants, and the participants are often too busy staying alive to notice anything but the terror of the moment. Once I was removed from the frontal impact of combat, if only by a few yards distance, the jolting reality of how things actually occurred dawned on me in all its glory. The scratchy voices that came at me through the radio brought new insight into the thought process of higher command. In many cases, I became convinced that there simply was no process at work there. I had seen a bit of this when I was yet a newcomer to the company.

In January 1970, we were blessed with a change of battalion commanders. This was nothing particularly new. The battalion was commanded by an officer holding the rank of lieutenant colonel, and it was a pretty standard practice to shift command every few months or so. I have no idea what the reasoning for that must have been. Just about the time a commander really got the feel for what was going on and how to best serve his men and the mission, he was shipped off and a newcomer took his place. In most wars this was a matter of promoting a combat-hardened man who had proven himself in that particular area of operation. The Vietnam conflict seems to have been an exception to that rule.

Since the war in Vietnam was not a declared war by definition, and since our combat forces were forbidden to cross into North Vietnam and put an end to the hostilities once and for all, the rules for just about everything changed accordingly. Men who had chosen the military for a profession used the assignment to combat command in Vietnam as a stepping-stone to promotion. Vietnam was jokingly referred to as a "light colonel's war." It was pretty well known that a lieutenant colonel needed to have a tour of duty as a combat commander under his belt if he aspired to the more prestigious rank of full colonel. This being the case, the command of combat battalions seemed to become a revolving-door affair, often bringing in new commanders who had no idea what was going on when they stepped into such a weighty position of leadership.

On the January morning that I first witnessed one of these changes of command, the company had been working along the edge of the Ho Bo Woods, a particularly nasty area. That morning we picked up everything and everybody and ran for the base camp of Cu Chi. Once there, we were assembled and the new battalion commander stood up on a track and addressed us. I can't remember a word he said, but an abridged version would probably be, "Hello, men. . . . I am the colonel. Now go back to work." We then loaded up and made our way right back to the place we had been before this nonsense was forced on us. On the way back out, one of the tracks hit a mine. It could have all been so easily and sensibly avoided.

From my position as a rifleman on the Two Zero track, I was not privy to the orders that came to us through battalion command. Generally, such directives never reached my ears, yet the consequences became evident. The change of command in January brought with it a number of new protocols in the way we were to operate as a company. This seems to be par for the course. New commanders evidently believe that if they don't make noticeable differences, they will not be credited with improving the combat effectiveness of their new command. Once again, the specter of promotion to colonel seemed to be looming in the background of such decisions.

In January it was passed down to the platoons that we were to make some drastic changes. The new policy dictated that we would open the top hatch of the tracks and all stand inside, with only the top half of our bodies sticking up. This was supposed to protect us from ambush fire and booby traps hung up in trees. Anyone who had spent much time on an APC knew how really silly and completely uncomfortable such an arrangement was. The tracks were all-terrain vehicles that bounced, bumped, swayed, and made standing up inside completely ludicrous.

The second change was a doozy. We were ordered to fill our tracks with Bangalore torpedoes and forty-pound explosive charges, to be used in destroying bunkers, tunnels, and enemy fortifications. The unfortunate effect of this was to make our tracks moving ammunition dumps. If we ran across even a small land mine, the possibility of setting off such weighty ordnance became very likely.

Rumor had it that all the company commanders in the battalion had presented their objections. Rumor aside, we loaded up with things that go boom, opened the hatches, crawled inside the tracks, and waited for disaster to strike. It would not be long, and it was not without loss, before the dire predictions came true. A track in one of the other companies hit a mine and left a burned-out hulk where the men had been. With a sudden stroke of command genius, orders came down from battalion that we were to return to the older, more reasonable mode of operation. In the emotionless manner of men who have no real choice in much of their fate, we accepted the confusing changes as a testament to the fierce ambition for promotion and moved on. Many months later, sitting in the gunner's hatch of the command track, passing along messages to Captain Meilstrup, I gained a new and depressing realization of just how much of the war was run by similar flights of foolishness.

The list of really stupid directives that came down to us from higher command was long and disheartening. Fortunately, the idiocy trickled in a little at a time, which softened the blow somewhat. While the company was assigned to work in War Zone C, near the Mekong River, we received a directive that instructed combat units operating within one thousand yards of the river not to fire unless they were fired on by the enemy. It then insisted that units contacting the enemy within five hundred yards of the river not fire! I have no idea how other units responded to this ridiculous order, but all of the soldiers of C Company became amazingly bad judges of distance.

Since I was no longer in a line platoon, I no longer went out on ambush patrol. Instead of spending those stressful nights lying in wait for what was to come out there in the darkness, I had become the scratchy, metallic voice that spoke to such men through the handset of the PRC–25 radio.

"Alpha Pappa One, Alpha Pappa One. This is Five Four Whiskey. I need a sit rep, over."

Many nights I had lain in the all-consuming Asian dark, pressing the handset of the radio close to my ear and responding to just such a request in hoarse whispered tones.

"Alpha Pappa One. I have negative sit rep at this time."

It seemed an odd twist of fate that I should find myself on the other side of such exchanges, no longer hiding in the dark with a small group of men who seemed terribly alone out there. I had become one of those who stayed within the protective circle of the tracks and kept watch over the ambush patrols by radio. I found that sometimes, I was the voice that sent them some of the absurdity that stung the average soldier with such blatant disregard. It must be remembered that Vietnam was not a declared war. It should also be noted that when the bullets and rockets began to fly in the dark of night, it was impossible for the line troop to tell the difference.

The United States as a whole had jumped in with both feet to support the troops and the mission of World War II. Many of us tend to believe such complete involvement by the American people in the nation's military endeavors is what Americans always do. A quick review of history would suggest otherwise. The full-out efforts of Americans on the home front during World War II was a rare exception rather than the rule.

Life back in the world, as the GI referred to home, seemed to go on as if the war in Vietnam were an afterthought. Oh, there were protests by college kids and splashes of combat footage on the evening news, but the business world seemed to trade on the exchange and jockey for position in the marketplace, as if what was happening on the other side of the globe was not happening to American troops in the field. This mercantile indifference sometimes cast a very long shadow.

The week had been long, and the ambush patrols from C Company had been many. The company was long overdue for a stand-down, inside base-camp wires, with all that such a period of rest means. My night watch at the radio was running as usual when we got a message from brigade, which is a step higher than battalion. The voice on the other end relayed the information with typical radio-operator detachment. We were simply told not to fire any more M-79 rounds than were absolutely necessary during engagement with enemy troops. This meant that our defensive probing fire with the M-79 grenade launcher was forbidden. Our defensive perimeter was generally protected from enemy troops sneaking up on us by intermittent fire from the "doopers," or grenade launchers. When I passed the message to Captain Meilstrup, he swore softly and grabbed the microphone, demanding to know why such an order had been issued. The answer was short and sweet. The voice on the other end of the radio told us there was a strike on back in the world, and they would not ship any more dooper rounds until somebody got more money, or a longer lunch break, or something important like that. Meilstrup shook his head, handed me the scribbled message, and said, "Tell 'em." I swallowed hard and pressed the transmit button on the mike. I am sure that somewhere, today, there is someone who was out there in the dark that night who heard my voice telling him not to shoot at the enemy with the M-79 unless he absolutely had to because somebody in Michigan wanted a better retirement package.

At that moment I felt that the world no longer made any sense at all. In retrospect, I believe it was one of the few moments in my life when I was absolutely right.

Track Twenty-One

CUE: *Fortunate Son*, CREEDENCE CLEARWATER REVIVAL

The black smoke rising just ahead of us gave dark testimony to what we were heading for. Company A, 1st of the 5th, was engaged with a sizable enemy force. I knew this because the chatter in my headset painted the picture pretty well. The men who were engaged in the fight had stumbled into a unit of the North Vietnamese Army, not guerrilla forces. These were well-equipped professional soldiers, and based on the fury of the fight they were putting up, their numbers seemed to be superior. Our Alpha Company had been looking for them and found exactly what it was after.

The Vietnamese commander had caught the tracks strung out in line and had lured them into a horseshoe-shaped attack. This was a textbook maneuver and was working exactly as it had been designed. The troops of

Alpha Company were fighting desperately to extricate themselves from a deadly situation, and we were speeding to their aide with all dispatch. The outcome of such a firefight was already determined by the strength of numbers. The Americans could simply pour in more and more men and equipment as they became available. It was an old tactic. It was how Ulysses S. Grant won battle after battle during the War between the States, yet such victories were pretty hard on the first troops into the fray. Alpha Company was the first, and reports of its losses came through the headset to me as we came within sight of the battle. As we stopped and waited for the rest of our company to draw up into the line of attack, the tracks of Alpha Company began to withdraw. They moved past us in broken order, with the line troops walking beside the vehicles. On top were laid the bodies of the killed and wounded. The first sergeant of Alpha Company was among the dead. There was something ominous in that. First sergeants were men who had survived long enough to reach that exalted rank by living through many such engagements, often in multiple wars. As the track bearing his dead body passed by us, I had a sinking feeling. It was an ill omen.

The good news was that the enemy fighters were already engaged and unable to redeploy their positions. We knew where they were. The bad news was that the only way to get at them and keep them from escaping into the Vietnamese countryside was to keep them engaged until air support showed up to cut off their way out. This meant we had to go right back in where Alpha Company had taken such a pounding. We had to go in there and either overrun them or keep them busy until the jets showed up. This was a new kind of war to me.

Everything I had been a part of up to this time had happened on ambush patrols at night or in flurried attacks
against obviously inferior forces. Now we were evenly
matched and heading into something altogether new.

Captain Meilstrup had dismounted from the command track and was engaged in a deep conversation with
the commander of Alpha Company. They poured over
the map of the area, and both pointed back at the still-
smoldering battleground. I noticed that our first sergeant, Sergeant Strain, walked over to the command
track of Alpha Company. The body of its first sergeant
was laid out over the trim vane and was covered with a
green army blanket. Sergeant Strain looked under the
blanket for a moment, then turned and walked back to
stand at the side of Captain Meilstrup. He did not look
back at the blanket-covered corpse again. Months later
and quite by accident, I learned that the two first sergeants had known each other for years and had served in
the same combat unit in the Korean conflict. I would
come to understand completely the sudden detachment
from one who had been a comrade in arms.

Meilstrup climbed aboard the command track and
took the headset from me. He gave terse orders of movement to the platoon leaders, and we started making our
way right back into the hornets' nest that had so banged
up Alpha Company. I checked the .50-caliber machine
gun to make sure it was ready to go. I moved boxes of
ammunition closer to me so I could reload with less
effort, then I gripped the handles of the gun with sweating fingers. This was different. We knew the North
Vietnamese were about to unload on us, yet we kept
moving forward. We had to engage them and keep them
from breaking up piecemeal and retreating across the

river into Cambodia. Our mortar tracks began to fire rounds behind the enemy lines to keep them from moving in that direction, and on we pressed, toward the front of their line.

We moved steadily, relentlessly toward the wood line in what seemed to be a slow-motion take in a movie, and then the blunt sound of a small explosion broke the silence. The time warp seemed to shift into high gear, and men and tracks moved faster, pressing the attack. My position as gunner on the command track usually left me as a nonshooting observer because our people were often in my line of fire. This time, as the line of battle spread out, I found myself in a clear area, and I pressed the butterfly trigger on the big machine gun. The fact that I could shoot back immediately settled my tension to a controllable level of battle nervousness. I was once more a fighting member of C Company. In retrospect, it seems kind of silly, but I have to say it made me feel better.

The fighting was heavy for about twenty minutes, then the enemy gave way. Our tracks overwhelmed their positions, and they simply melted away. As the last shots were being fired, I saw two men bearing a blanket-shrouded stretcher toward us. The body they carried was heavy, but they lifted the stretcher high and slid it onto the flat deck behind my gunner's hatch. It would be our duty to carry the corpse back to the resupply point, where it would be sent back to graves registration in the rear. Captain Meilstrup was still directing the mop-up action using my headset. He looked over his shoulder at the shrouded stretcher and asked me to see who it was. This meant I was to check the dog tags. This was not a usual part of my duty as the gunner. In fact, I can only remember having to do this one other time, in another country. It was during a similar heated engagement across the Mekong River in Cambodia. On that day, as the stretcher was lifted into place on the deck of the track, I reached behind me and pulled up the edge of the blanket. The face underneath the green wool was devoid of expression and stared back at me with sightless eyes. It was Oscar Solis.

It dawns on me now that after I replaced the dirty green wool of the army blanket over his lifeless face, I did not allow myself conscious thoughts of him for almost thirty years, when I saw his name on a granite memorial to fallen Texas veterans. It was an intense moment, filled with all the emotion I could not afford on that hot day in 1970. I have often wondered how many such moments the veterans of multiple wars, like 1st Sergeant Strain, must have gone through.

Track Twenty-Two

CUE: *Signs*, FIVE MAN ELECTRICAL BAND

As anybody who has ever been in a modern army can testify, there must be a covert-operations unit somewhere, probably in a secret office in the Pentagon, that does nothing but think up ridiculous signs that confirm the notion that the average GI has no native intelligence at all. This is most obviously confirmed by the raised and boldly printed letters on the front of a Claymore mine, which plainly read Front Toward Enemy. If this still leaves some doubt as to the upper echelon's opinion of the decision-making capabilities of the average line troop, all one has to do is look at the back of the Claymore. Printed there, in the same raised characters, is the word *back*.

I suppose every walk of life needs a certain amount of written direction. Signs are the most elementary form of such necessary instruction. Signs bear directions and information such as Stop, Walk, Don't Walk, No Smoking, No Trespassing, and, my personal favorite, Clothing-Optional Beach. Military installations are no exception to the signs rule. In fact, they may be more prone to the penchant for printed directives than civilian organizations. Mine Field, Keep Out would be a good example.

The first army sign I remember seeing the day I was inducted was hand-lettered on a piece of white poster board hanging over a water fountain. The bold lettering announced: Do Not Expectorate in Fountain.

Signs were everywhere in an army base. There must have been a huge contingent of men assigned to each unit to do nothing but paint signs. There were signs announcing unit headquarters, complete with artwork. There were signs indicating where to go and where not to go. There were signs reminding the local inhabitants of personal hygiene and the protocols of military courtesy. There were even signs telling you what you could and could not discuss. If this were not enough, in Vietnam one had to learn the meanings of signs written in a foreign tongue, such as Cam Vao. This was a general warning to keep out of an area that had been mined or booby-trapped. It was a good thing to know if you had any ambition of going home with your body mostly intact. There were signs everywhere, yet I must admit to never having seen anybody actually painting a sign.

Once in the field, signs became more of a source of personal expression for most American units. In the mechanized companies there were no barracks or buildings, so the tracks themselves became the bearers of art and ingenuity. Much like the nose art on aircraft from past wars, painted designs and sayings appeared on the sides and machine-gun shields of the armored personnel carriers. Such artistic expressions were often as much the opinion of the men onboard as the name of the track. I remember one that declared in boldly painted letters, "If it eats rice, shoot it!"

When I was assigned to the mountaintop relay station of Nui Ba Den, a steep path led up to the orderly room in the old pagoda. The path wound its way through heavy boulders on which were painted sayings you could read as you ascended: "Remember the Alamo. Remember the Maine. Remember Pearl Harbor. Try to forget Nui Ba Den." Everyone who had ever been on that godforsaken mountain seemed to have scribbled his name on the rock below this last sentiment. I wonder if the communists or the weather have washed away all those names.

Signs are not always words painted on something. In a war zone they are often much more subtle, but just as revealing. Little things told you a great deal about a man, without his ever saying a word.

The uniform in Vietnam was called jungle, or tropical, fatigues. The sleeves were made to be rolled up or left down, and the pants had huge pockets that were intended to be useful to a man who must haul everything he needs to sustain life. The boots were made for life in a hot and terribly wet environment. They had metal plates in the soles to deflect sharpened bamboo stakes, and screened vent holes were included to let the monsoon water drain out. The boots had black leather toes and heels, but the rest of the footgear was made of a green material that would hold up to the strain of infantry life. The odd part of it was that only 10 percent of the troops in Vietnam were combat troops, yet all of them wore the same boots, pants, and shirts. It was the way in which these uniforms were worn that became a sign of the men who wore them.

The required headgear for men who served in the rear echelon was the green GI baseball cap. Infantry troops were forbidden to wear such caps. Aside from the battle-worn steel helmets, the infantry soldier wore the bush, or boonie, hat. The mech-unit soldiers often ran a wire from the C-ration boxes through the seam of the brim and placed stiff ovals of cardboard, from those same C-ration boxes, into the crown, causing the bush hat to have a particularly rakish look. It was a sign that they were cavalry troops.

A man's fatigues faded with his time out in the sun. The longer a man had been in-country, the more faded his fatigues became. It was a sign of experience. When new guys came to the unit as replacements, their fresh green fatigues stood out as a mark of their inexperience. Similarly, the boots of a line troop set him apart from others.

The rear-echelon troops, working in offices and warehouses in the base camps, were held to a rule of military decorum that the troops of the mechanized units could not be. The garrison troops were inspected and regulated as to haircuts and shined boots and all the normal military trappings of soldiering. The mech soldiers were recognizable at a glance by the very absence of such military cleanliness. Living constantly beyond the wire, the mech units simply could not comply with the regimented dress code of other units, and so their somewhat earthy appearance became a sign of their service.

Those troops who did duty in the base camps and reached the mark of having less than thirty days left to go on their tours graduated to that revered status of being short timers. Many of them would carry a specially made baton or swagger stick that was a sign they were close to going home. This revered symbol was called a short timer's stick. No short timer sticks were carried in the field. Time in-country was kept by each man on a small calendar, and the only mark of his extended time in the line was a subtle yet discernable look in his eyes, sometimes called the thousand-yard stare. The look defies description, yet is unforgettable to any who have seen it. The truly odd phenomenon is that combat soldiers from many wars have testified to recognizing the look in others, yet none of them ever admits to having seen it in himself. Perhaps this is a sign as well.

Track Twenty-Three

CUE: *Riders on the Storm*, THE DOORS

The days had stretched long, and the nights seemed to go on without end. C Company had been out for months without a break. The mechanized companies that stayed out in the field were supposed to be given stand-down times. These were two- and three-day breaks from action in which the company could enter the base camps to refit the machines of war and rest the troops. It was a time when those who lived life in the bush could take real showers, drink a beer or two, and sleep in an actual bed. Three months had passed since the company had been inside the base camp wires for a night. Promises for stand down kept coming from battalion command, but we were simply handed new orders and new areas of operation instead. We were beginning to become a bit the worse for wear. I remember one day when the com-

pany met another mechanized unit from the 2nd
Battalion of the 22nd Infantry (Mech) on the road. They
were in clean uniforms, and their tracks all looked as if
they had just come through a car wash. In comparison,
we looked very much like members of the Hells Angels,
caked with trail dust, some wearing headbands and sunglasses, with hair and mustaches untrimmed and
uncombed. It was a stark reminder of how long we had
been out.

The rumors of the coming incursion into Cambodia
had buzzed through all of Vietnam via the jungle
grapevine. Everyone knew it was going to happen. Our
group sincerely hoped we would finally be pulled out of
the field and given a stand down, rather than having to
charge off into another country looking for the NVA.

The radio messages from the higher-ups became more
and more secure and were often only for the ears of
Captain Meilstrup. Those of us on the command track
had a sneaking suspicion we were about to be thrown
into the invasion mix. To our joy, one night Meilstrup
emerged from the track after receiving one of those "ears
only" messages from the colonel and announced we were
not going to Cambodia. It seemed the headquarters types
had finally noticed how long C Company had been out
and were giving us a break. We were to go south into the
Renegade Woods to secure it for the engineers who
were engaged in pulling down that formidable forest.
Then we were to be sent back to the base camp of Tay
Ninh for a well-deserved stand down.

This was terrific news. While the rest of the battalion
was involved in refitting and preparing to cross the
Mekong River in a general invasion of the NVA strongholds in Cambodia, we were to have the relatively easy

job of guarding a bunch of bulldozers for a week or two. After that, we would finally get a couple of days inside the wire. The morale of the company jumped tremendously, and we settled into the routine of making sure the engineers didn't get shot. I can't tell you why, but during this stint of duty, I had a gnawing feeling that something was about to drop on our heads.

The message that came over the secure set was for the ears of Captain Meilstrup only. We all exited the track, and for a long time the captain was alone, talking over the rushing frequencies that could only be tuned in by those who had the same secure setup on the other end. When he came out, he told us to take a walk so he could talk with the first sergeant for a moment. We strayed off a little distance in the darkness and stood shuffling our feet and dreading what was being discussed. After a short time, Meilstrup started off in the direction of the other tracks, and 1st Sergeant Strain motioned us back. What he said caused our hearts to sink: "We're going to Cambodia."

The other invasion units had all been preparing for several weeks. Each company was brought into the base camps, the troops rested and the equipment refitted or replaced in anticipation of heavy action. Then the invasion companies were moved east to a staging area along the big river. There they camped and waited until the go order was issued. This seemed to have been true of all units except C Company, 1st of the 5th. Our case seemed to have been different.

We were unceremoniously plucked from our mission of securing the engineers in the Renegade Woods and flung on the road to the Tay Ninh base camp. We assumed we would get the same treatment as all the other units. We looked forward to a few days' rest and recreation inside the wire while the tracks and weapons were made ready for invasion. This turned out to be a misconception. As we neared Tay Ninh, we halted along the side of the road, and a small army of resupply people came out, bringing us fuel, food, and more ammunition than we had ever had at one time. We never even got close to going inside the base-camp wire. In a couple of hours, we were back on the road and charging straight for the staging area. Stand down had once again proven to be an unrealized dream, and now what lay ahead of us was the first combat invasion of a foreign country by US troops since the end of the Korean War.

Dark was closing when we pulled into the staging area. It was a huge congregation of APC units from all over. Some of them appeared to have been waiting for days. We were the last to get there. Tired, threadbare, and stretched to the limits of endurance, C Company, 1st of the 5th, went into its defensive circle and settled in for the night. At 3:00 a.m., a hand shook me from an exhausted sleep. It was Captain Meilstrup. He instructed me to pass along the order for the company to load up and prepare to move out. We were to be the point element of the invasion.

I have often reflected on this moment. There we were, a combat company that had spent an extended amount of time out in the bush without a break. We were a combat company that had not been sent into the base camps to rest and get ready for this major offensive. We were the very last unit to arrive at the staging area, where some had been waiting for days. All this was true, and yet we were making our way toward the river, in the early morning darkness, as the spearhead of the invasion force. It was incomprehensible, and yet, it was somewhat of a compliment. Tired as we were, the men at the top had chosen us to be the first into the fray.

Track Twenty-Four

CUE: *Run through the Jungle,*
CREEDENCE CLEARWATER REVIVAL

The inky blackness of the night seemed to envelop us as the company snaked out onto the dirt road leading to the river. In that early morning darkness, the rumble of the engines seemed more pronounced for some reason. It was a chorus of deep, subdued power, which waited to be unleashed. I assumed everyone knew we were taking a road that would lead us onto the pages of history books. Even if they were not so historically minded, it was impossible to not feel the anticipation in every man. After years of playing around the edges of what the world was afraid to call a war, we were finally taking the force of our military power into the backyard of the enemy. Word had come to us of similar crossings to the south, which had sent the NVA reeling before the

American lines. Now it was our turn to cross the river into a Cambodian region where our intelligence had placed the NVA headquarters. As we inched along the road, behind the mine-sweeping teams, the tension consumed us.

The trees on either side of the darkened road reached high into the night sky. I couldn't tell how thick the woods were beyond the edge of the dirt road. It could have been a forest big enough to hide whole armies, but that was not what really worried me. What tugged at the elbow of my thoughts was the shadowy specter of the men walking in front of the tracks. Their dark figures moved relentlessly onward, waving their electronic devices over the surface of the road. In their awkward and terribly slow way, they were making sure the ground before us had not been prepared for disaster by the enemy. As they preceded us through the gloom, I found myself looking back over my shoulder again and again. The sun would rise behind us, and we had to be at the river before dawn.

Captain Meilstrup was keeping his own thoughts as the time ran and our progress remained interminably slow. Suddenly he stood up from his seat beside my gunner's hatch and looked behind us at the still-dark sky. He held out his hand to me and formed a fist. It was a sign I knew well. I hit the microphone button and called the company to a halt. We called the mine-sweeping team in, and Meilstrup had me call the platoon leaders to our track.

When the three lieutenants stood beside our track, looking up at us from the darkness, Captain Meilstrup reached over into the hatch where I kept the tommy gun. My bush hat was there, hung over the muzzle of that vintage weapon. The hat had a number of hand grenade pins woven into the looped hatband. The captain took three of the grenade rings from my hat. He bent the retaining pin of one of the rings double, making it the shortest of the three. He placed the pins in his fist, leaving only three rings sticking out, and leaned down toward the waiting lieutenants. The platoon leaders looked at each other, then each reached up and picked a ring. Lieutenant Phillips from 2nd Platoon had taken the short pin.

In curt, military terms, Meilstrup explained that the mine sweeping would take too long. We had to be at the river before first light, so we were going to bust the road. The faces of the platoon leaders were hard to read in the dark, but each of them knew what was to be done. The company would run for the river along a road that was most probably mined. Meilstrup pointed his finger at Phillips and said, in very flat command tones:

"Phillips, you're lead track. I'm right behind you. The rest of you pull in behind us and spread out your tracks fifty yards apart, so if they hit a mine they won't take anyone else with them. We'll be moving fast, so try to keep your interval."

The idling of the engines was suddenly very deep in the still night. The three young officers looked at each other and awkwardly shook hands, then turned and walked off into the darkness. I have often wondered what they said to each other. I still wonder if Phillips kept that mutilated hand grenade pin that had placed him at the point of an invasion.

Carnes, our driver, pulled us out of line and moved us to the place where we would fall in line behind Phillips's lead track. When all the platoons reported to be ready, we started for the river. The company spread out and accelerated to as much speed as the twisting dirt road and the early morning dimness would allow. All I remember about that ride is that no one on the track said a word until, without incident, we pulled up to the river and the pontoon bridge that spanned it. We arrived just as the first light of morning filtered through the trees.

The bridge floated and bobbed in the current that was the watery border between nations. It had been prepared by the engineers and guarded by ARVN and Special Forces troops, who now watched us curiously as we carefully inched the heavy tracks over the floating highway. Phillips's track was first across, and one of his boys reached out and stuck a crudely printed sign on a tree with the stab of a bayonet. We were still the second track in line, and as we crossed the pontoon bridge and drove onto dry ground, I could read the hand-printed message. It said, plainly, "Welcome to Cambodia, 1/5 (Mech)." Irony strikes people at the oddest moments. Maybe that's what makes it ironic. At that moment, I recalled how many times during the past months I had wished I was somewhere other than Vietnam, and now I was.

Once across the river, we pulled over and deployed to cover the crossings of several other companies. When that was accomplished, we started out along a well-traveled dirt road that led us beyond the river and into a rich agricultural bottomland. The place was amazingly beautiful compared to Vietnam, which was just across the river. The rice fields were well kept, and the dikes were trimmed and neat, not unlike the curbed yards in an American suburb. Making a comparison between the pristine beauty of the Cambodian farmland and the bedraggled appearance of the Vietnamese countryside was unfair. Vietnam had been embroiled in one war after another for four decades, and the whole country seemed to be held together with chewing gum and kite string. Cambodia had remained pretty much untouched. As the lines of olive-drab military monsters made their way down the tree-shaded road, it was obvious that the situation had changed.

We expected the enemy to engage us at any moment, yet we moved deeper and deeper into Cambodian territory without a hint of resistance. We passed ox carts and old, French-made trucks that had been abandoned along the path of our march. It was a sign that there had been a surprised retreat of the general population, which was unaware of what was happening. It meant no news broadcasts or information of any kind had been disseminated to the farming communities that dotted the landscape near the river. Because of public announcements by President Nixon and the ambitious reporting of almost everyone in the broadcast news industry, the entire world must have known that American troops were storming across the river into NVA-held areas of Cambodia. The world knew what was happening, but the local farmers seemed to have been kept in the dark. They didn't know we were coming until we showed up in their front yards.

Another fact struck us, pretty early on. Though we saw all sorts of civilian signs along the roadside, we saw nothing of the North Vietnamese Army. This was somewhat unsettling. It either meant it was not there or it had performed an orderly pullback and was preparing a reception for us somewhere up ahead. Just as we were beginning to worry, something happened that changed our minds about the preparedness of the local NVA.

We pulled off the road and into a large open area that was lined with terribly tall palm trees. A small village could be seen in the distance, across the open fields. Meilstrup sent out recon tracks to check along the wood line and then started the company moving slowly in the direction of the village. We had not gone a hundred yards when the captain called a halt. One of the tall palm trees was immediately to our right. There, in the thin strip of shade provided by the trunk of the tall tree, sat an NVA backpack with an army pith helmet resting upon it. The pack and the helmet were retrieved and inspected. The equipment was new and without any signs of wear. The owner must have been lying in the limited shade of the tree when he heard our approach and ran for cover. We realized he was probably hiding in the surrounding wood line, watching us at that very moment.

We began to move again, a bit more cautiously this time, when we came across another of the packs. It, too, rested beneath one of the tall palm trees. It was then that we noticed that there was a pack and a helmet beneath every palm tree in sight. At that moment, a single rifle shot was fired at us from the wood line, and the action began.

Groups of NVA soldiers rose up from behind rice dikes, where they were hiding, and made attempts to run for the cover of the woods. Speeding tracks and heavy machine guns cut them off, making dead men and taking prisoners. Squads of APCs swept the woods with concentrated .50-caliber fire, and what resistance had been initiated from such cover melted away. Enemy soldiers seemed to be running everywhere. They appeared to be completely without discipline or intelligent command and bent only on escape. The whole incident was

over in a few minutes, and we converged on the tiny village, surrounding it and throwing out recon platoons
into the nearby woods. It was an attempt to again establish contact with the fleeing enemy.

The radio hummed in my headset with all sorts of
reports and requests, but by now, Meilstrup had dismounted the command track and was moving on the
ground through the village. He was communicating by
the use of the PRC–25 radios, carried by his two RTOs.
I was simply sitting in the gunner's hatch, listening to the
mop-up action, when something hard hit my helmet. I
was convinced that someone was shooting at me when a
second missile hit my shoulder, and I found that it was a
small pebble. I turned to discover that 1st Sergeant Strain
was tossing rocks at me to get my attention. He
motioned for me to get down off the track and follow
him. I was a bit confused, but I grabbed the tommy gun
and made my way to the ground.

I followed the top kick through the village and around
the corner of a large stone building, which turned out to
be the local Buddhist temple. There we found Captain
Meilstrup, towering over a small monk who was
wrapped in the traditional orange robe and looking at
Meilstrup as if he had three heads. As we approached, the
captain was using a combination of crude sign language
and broken English to make himself understood by the
diminutive monk.

"Are there many . . . beaucoup . . . ti ti . . . NVA? You
understand NVA? . . . North Vietnamese? . . . We are
American. . . . You know American?"

The captain's face showed real frustration, and the vis-
age of the orange-clad holy man showed nothing but
confusion. Meilstrup shook his head and turned to me,

asking, "Stoney, didn't you say you took French in college?" I nodded, and the captain ordered me to see if I could get through to the monk. It was not an odd request, since the whole of Southeast Asia had been French Indochina at one time.

"Parlez-vous Francais?"

I felt awkward as the words came from my mouth, especially since I had all but flunked French in college. I pointed to myself and intoned, "Je suis American."

The little monk looked at me with a sort of uncomfortable silence. His eyes kept darting to the huge muzzle of the tommy gun and then back to my face. It was obvious he had no idea what I had just asked him and wasn't quite sure whether I intended to shoot him or not. I looked at the captain and shook my head. Meilstrup shook his head and resumed the futile attempt to communicate through exaggerated gestures and fractured sentences.

"How many? . . . Many . . . NVA . . . North Vietnamese . . . How many NVA here? . . . How many . . . here?"

At this point the tiny monk opened his mouth and spoke with a clipped British accent that sounded for all the world like Prince Charles.

"Oh, I don't know, perhaps a thousand."

The silent moment that followed was all but comical. When Meilstrup recovered from his shock, he asked in amazed tones, "You speak English?"

The small monk smiled indulgently and retorted, "Yes, but I was beginning to wonder about that."

On that hot afternoon, filled with confusion and the sounds of war, the sarcastic wisdom of George Bernard Shaw had raised its head once again. It was Shaw who had observed that the English and the Americans are two peoples separated by a common language.

Track Twenty-Five

CUE: *Whole Lotta Shakin' Going On,*
JERRY LEE LEWIS

It seemed every unit that crossed the border found itself chasing a fleeing enemy. The obvious fact that the NVA was involved in a headlong but staggered retreat from its former established positions was encouraging, but a bit confusing. It was running off and leaving all sorts of supplies and munitions that had been hand carried to these locations from North Vietnam. What we began to stumble into was amazing.

For several days, we made sporadic contact with the enemy, which always ended with them breaking off the combat and melting farther back into the wooded countryside. Then one morning my headset buzzed with reports from our point element that it had found some bunkers. As it turned out, it had not just found some bunkers, it had stumbled into the entire headquarters complex of the North Vietnamese Army.

We moved carefully to determine the size of the complex and were astounded to discover that the bunkers stretched for hundreds of yards. It was truly a base camp, underground. There were hospital bunkers, complete with primitive operating rooms. There were arms bunkers, still filled with RPGs and explosives. There were classrooms and map rooms and even offices wired with field telephones. We found everything from huge stores of rice to intelligence that had been gathered and hand carried across the river from Vietnam.

As the men from the Intelligence Corps were going through the plastic bags filled with captured American maps and documents, one of them pulled out a pair of American dog tags and read aloud the name stamped on them.

"Sgt. Dan O. Collins."

To his surprise, the intelligence officer heard a reply from just outside the bunker.

"Yeah."

As it turned out, Dan Collins was the radio operator for the artillery forward observer who was assigned to C Company. Collins had lost his dog tags somewhere in the Michelin rubber plantation in February. At that moment, he was standing just outside a large hole in the ground, in another country, where army intelligence people had just pulled those same dog tags out of a mildewed plastic bag. The whole incident seemed like an episode from the TV show *Ripley's Believe It or Not*.

With the find of this major cache of weapons and information, we all thought that our company would stop and guard the area while the intelligence types did their thing. As usual, the surmising of the men of C Company was in error. The chore of guarding the captured NVA headquarters was taken over by another mechanized company, and we were thrown, once again, into the search for the retreating enemy.

Charging off through the tall trees, we were unaware of how the news of our invasion had played out before the rest of the world. As is so often the case with American politics, this move into Cambodia had its fans and its detractors. People who had sons fighting in Vietnam wanted the war to come to an end and their sons to be safe from the NVA, which had been protected from American attack in the sanctuaries of Cambodia. These folks were applauding President Nixon for his bold move to deny the enemy its safe haven. Those who were against the military action in Vietnam and were protesting in various ways already, protested this new action as well. Such a split in the political firmament had a way of causing the powers that be to seek new and even more disgusting ways to cover their political behinds. As it turned out, Nixon was no exception.

As C Company, 1st of the 5th, made its way deeper and deeper into the Cambodian countryside, the word came to us that Nixon had appeared on international television and announced that US forces had, indeed, pressed across the Mekong River into Cambodia. He then declared that US troops would not penetrate beyond a certain point into that country. Essentially what he had done was to draw a line on the map and tell the enemy that if it could scamper back behind this line on the map, the big, bad Americans would not touch it. That explained why the enemy was abandoning everything and retreating so completely. All it had to do was fall back behind the safe lines and it would be secure to regroup and press attacks on our forces from strongholds we were forbidden to attack. It was Vietnam all over again.

The line of our tracks was moving through a sparsely wooded area when the landscape began to change. The forest grew dense and the trees became larger, stretching high into the sky. This was not a good area for tracked vehicles. The big trees limited the avenue of movement for the APCs, and the increased height of such vegetation made air support difficult. For a smaller force to attack a larger one, it was important to find ground where air support was difficult or impossible to use. The aggressors would then have to get in close enough to engage the enemy so that artillery could not be called into play for fear of hitting friendly troops. It was an ideal spot for a sizable ambush, which is exactly what occurred. It might have worked had it not been for a mechanical malfunction that happened at exactly the right spot.

George Bradley had recently become the driver of the Two Four track. As he urged the machine through the woods, a track block came loose, and the APC was halted in place to await repair. The rest of the company moved forward, slipping neatly into a rather large horseshoe of concealed NVA troops—a favorite tactic of the enemy and one we had encountered before. When the firing began, the enemy sent troops to close the end of the horseshoe and surround us. Instead, they ran into Bradley and the men of the Two Four track, who put up a whale of a fight and kept the ambush from closing around us.

The attack opened with a sharp explosion that killed Oscar Solis. RPGs crippled the lead track, and the company returned fire with everything we had. Those of us who were .50-caliber gunners chewed up the surrounding wood line with such heavy fire that the enemy could not move toward us. We needed to back out of the ambush area to a distance that would be out of range of the enemy weapons but well within the reach of our heavy machine guns and mortars. The fact that the Two Four track was holding open the door for such a withdrawal gave us the ability to move out of the ambush zone and then strike again on ground of our own choosing. We had taken the element of surprise away from the enemy.

We gathered our killed and wounded and made the move just before the sun set. The night that followed was tense and filled with anticipation of an attack in the dark. Such an attack did not materialize. With the coming of the morning sun, we saddled up and prepared to press the enemy again. We entered the area of the conflict from the day before and spread out in attack formation. We made our way closer and closer to the line where the NVA had been entrenched the afternoon before. I gripped the handles of the machine gun and tried hard not to let anyone see how much I was thinking about the bullet marks that adorned the heavy steel shield of my gunner's hatch. I hadn't noticed any fire being directed at me during the previous attack. I hadn't even noticed the bullet marks until we neared the place of the former day's action. Suddenly I did notice, and with the notice came the fear.

The steady drone of the diesel engine seemed to rumble up my spine. I looked to my left at Carnes, who seemed perfectly calm. He seemed, in fact, like a man taking the family car on a Sunday drive, rather than a soldier pressing his APC into the face of a certain melee with North Vietnamese regulars. It caused me to try to look as relaxed as I possibly could. It was an act that was terribly transparent to anyone who saw my face.

Steadily onward we moved. Slowly but surely we advanced into the face of the enemy. We pressed forward until we reached the spot where they had been before, and pushed beyond that. We kept a slow, steady pace until we cleared the trees and came to a wide open meadow, where we halted. The North Vietnamese were gone. There was no sign of them. They had evidently slipped out during the night and left the area to us.

After much air reconnaissance and some probing around by recon units, it became obvious that the NVA had been fighting a delaying action with us. They were willing to expose themselves to superior firepower in a desperate effort to slow us down. We began to wonder what they may have been protecting. What was in our path that they had to protect?

The intelligence people flew in and out of our area repeatedly. They checked the dead enemy soldiers and asked us a bunch of questions that made very little sense, then came to the conclusion that a radar sighting of an unidentified aircraft, which had landed and taken off near our position during the night, was the answer to this puzzle. They assumed that the NVA had been protecting something or someone until they were able to get one of their few aircraft into the area and safely remove this prize. Whether it was true or not, the fact remains that after the mysterious aircraft left the area, the troops in front of us simply melted away into the countryside.

Track Twenty-Six

CUE: *The Party's Over*, WILLIE NELSON

The company was moving, once again, through an area not well suited for APCs. The woods were thick all about us, and our ability to maneuver was severely restricted. We had been sent on a search for enemy troops who were reported hiding just beyond the veil of forest. The higher-ups had detected radio signals coming from that area and had dispatched C Company to sniff it out.

Everyone was nervous about moving through the wooded area. Captain Meilstrup had thrown out flankers into the thickets to alert us to possible trouble in the making. This paid off in the long run. Word came to us from these hidden scouts that we were being followed. An ambush group was set up from our lead platoon, and they lay in wait as the company passed by. Sure enough, after the last tracks had passed the hidden ambush troops, a group of four NVA came along pushing bicycles in the ruts left by our tracked vehicles. A short skirmish ensued that killed all four of the enemy. This was unfortunate. We had hoped that at least one of them could have been taken alive. Such a captive might have provided us with valuable intelligence about what we were walking into. As it turned out, it might have made a difference to me personally.

While we stopped to report on the ambush results, a stranger walked up to the command track. His was a face I had never seen before. His fatigues were pretty clean, and he had camera equipment hung all over his body. He introduced himself as an army photographer, and as it turned out, he had been hitchhiking on one of the platoon tracks for a day or so. He had evidently been recording the invasion on film, by means of portraits taken of combat troops in the field. He talked with Meilstrup for a moment or so and was given permission to ride with us. He climbed onboard and set about taking all sorts of shots of Carnes, Meilstrup, 1st Sergeant Strain, and even some of me. I was kind of flattered that he was giving me so much attention, until I realized it wasn't me he was so fascinated with. I was still wearing the battered helmet Joe Raber had on the night an enemy round put a hole in it. The photographer took the helmet and began to hang it on first this thing and then that, trying to get the perfect framing for a wartime photograph with the tracks in the background. He was completely absorbed in getting just the right picture. I don't think he had any real appreciation of what a truly dangerous situation he had walked into. I don't think he ever did.

The knowledge that we were being tracked by the enemy changed the tactics somewhat. Meilstrup looked at the maps of the area and decided to get clear of the trees as fast as possible so we could operate to our best advantage if push came to shove. We began to move cautiously toward that aim when a huge explosion shook the ground ahead of us.

One of the APCs traveling with us was a "flame track." On it was mounted a huge flame thrower that could spit fire for hundreds of yards. It was the flame track that had blown up, several tracks ahead of us. The entire company went into combat mode. We thought, at first, that a rocket had taken out the flame track, and we spun to face either side of the trail and bring our guns to bear. I could hear the medics yelling as they assessed the human damage, and then I heard silence. For what seemed like a painfully long time, the entire company waited, with fingers on triggers, for the rest of the attack. Nothing happened. Meilstrup ordered men to penetrate the wood line on either side of the trail. They found no sign of an enemy. They did find the cable and detonator of a mine.

Once we realized that the flame track had been destroyed by a mine, rather than an RPG, it was understood what we needed to do. We blew up what was left of the flame track, loaded the wounded onto the medic's track, and started once again for the area outside of the trees. As we moved along, watching the wood line for enemy activity, I remember looking over the side of the track at the scorched hole where the flame track had been destroyed by the enemy mine. It was the last conscious memory I would have for more than twenty-four hours.

From this point on, the narrative of what happened the rest of that day will not be from my own recollections but rather from the recountings of a number of others who were present and involved. My memories of what happened, so long ago, have never returned.

The command track was completely disabled in one large explosion. Inspection after the fact discovered that the APC had been the victim of a Russian-made antitank mine that had been command detonated. That simply means someone saw us coming and had pulled the trigger. We were actually very lucky. The track was a complete combat loss, but there was only one fatality. It was the photographer who had so innocently hitched a ride with us to get close pictures of the war. The rest of the crew members, however, were pretty banged up. I was in that banged up category but evidently was not aware of it.

One of the other APCs hooked onto the immobilized hulk of the command track with chains and began to drag it from the wooded area. The rest of us walked out of the forest. The guys from the 2nd Platoon came over and picked me up. They have since told me that I was stiff and unable to crawl up onto the track but didn't complain of anything more than that. This surprised them a bit, since they had seen both me and Carnes fly high into the air from the force of the blast.

When the company cleared the woods, it went into a defensive circle. The command track had been dragged to the center of the circle but was pretty much useless. Even the radios were not working. I must have shown up there, for according to 1st Sergeant Strain, I was sent over to the medic's track to call in resupply and dustoff helicopters for the wounded. In the middle of transmitting the information to battalion, I evidently put the microphone down and climbed outside the track to relieve myself. When the disgruntled first sergeant stormed over to find out what the hell I was doing, he discovered that the stream of liquid coming from my body was bright red with blood. When he asked me if I was all right, I must have given him an empty-eyed stare and told him I was fine. He took me to the medics, and they began to peel my clothes back, finding that I was pretty banged up after all.

I was out of the game of transmitting radio calls, or anything else. I was making almost no sense at all, so they sat me down on the ramp of the medic's track and put a tag on me that described my injuries. When the dustoff choppers finally got there, I was loaded on. I have only one memory from that afternoon—at least I think it is a memory. It may only be a dream or a trick of my subconscious. I can remember the feel of the helicopter as its prop bit into the heavy air and began to lift us from the ground. I can hear the blades even now, as the flat slapping sound raised us higher and higher and then swung us over in a graceful arc above the trees. I seem to remember looking down on the defensive circle of the tracks and the strained faces of those I had served with as they looked up at the medevac bird. Then the chopper leveled off and I could see them no more. I cannot be sure it is a memory, but if it is, it was my last look at C Company, 1st of the 5th, as a combat unit in the field. What had happened to me would change my course as a soldier. What happened to them, the next morning, would change C Company.

Track Twenty-Seven

CUE: *Suicide is Painless*, NICK DRAKE

I cannot be sure when I actually came around. I think my mind began transmitting messages to my conscious state sometime on the afternoon of the next day. The mental cobwebs suddenly retreated, and I found myself laid out on a narrow bunk in a hospital ward. Larry Vunak, the gunner on the Two Four track, was seated at the foot of the bed talking with me. It became obvious that we had been talking for some time, but I had no idea what had been said. I also had no idea where I was. I looked about me to see if there might be bars on the windows and NVA guards at the door, but all I found were wounded GIs in blue pajamas. Vunak was an exception to that. He was still wearing combat fatigue pants and an olive-green T-shirt. As he talked to me, I began to notice that his shirt was covered with tiny flakes of metal. It looked almost as if he were covered with glitter. There were even flakes of metal in his hair. I am sure I asked him to explain, but about that time the cobwebs closed in around me again and the luxury of memory was lost to the ages once more.

Later that night the mists had cleared, and I was once again cranking out my normally poor level of actual thought. I discovered I was in the evac hospital in Tay Ninh base camp. I was told, probably for the fortieth time, that I had a ruptured right kidney and almost every muscle in my body was strained from the force of the explosion. My response was, "What explosion?" This was information outside the realm of the medical staff. I would have to wait to find out what had happened to me, and what had befallen the rest of the company the next morning.

The medical types smiled and told me I should be quiet and not move around too much until the soreness went away. This prescription was easy to follow. I could barely move at all, and when I did, it felt as if my entire body and been pounded thoroughly by a huge giant with a sledgehammer. Actually, that was not too far from the truth. Vunak came back to see me later that night. He had changed into a new set of jungle fatigues and no longer wore the T-shirt bedecked with glittering metal shavings. When I asked him about that, he launched into a description of what had happened the morning after I had been dusted off.

At dawn on May 12, C Company was hit with a huge attack from NVA forces. They were mortared and hit with RPGs in the dim, early morning light. The fight was tremendous, and the company held out against huge odds until reinforcements reached them and the NVA once again melted into the forest.

My questions were many—about who had gotten hit and what shape the company was in—but Vunak was unsure about any of that. He had been dusted off from the attack site after being in the thick of the fight. It suddenly dawned on me that the glittering metal that had been clinging to his T-shirt was shrapnel and metal fibers from an explosion. It would be some time before I was able to piece together what had happened. When I did get the truth, it was not good.

On the morning of May 12, 1970, C Company faced what could have been a battalion-sized attack by NVA forces. Six APCs were lost, five men were killed, and over forty were wounded. Later, through the GI grapevine, I would discover that Lester Lorig had received mortar fragments through his lung and was dusted off in very serious condition. He was taken first to Tay Ninh, then was shipped to Cu Chi, and eventually out to Japan by way of Bien Hoa Air Base.

C Company had taken a tremendous hit. It had survived and fought back with a vengeance, but after the morning of May 12, it was battered, understrength, and not really a fighting combat company in the true sense of the word. This group, which had stayed in the field for so long without rest or actual repair, was finally going to be sent back for a stand down. Just as I had not been a part of the early morning attack, I would not be included in what happened at the stand down in Tay Ninh. I was a patient in the 12th Evacuation Hospital in Cu Chi base camp.

The hospital comprised a series of Quonset huts laid out in line. The ward in which I was a patient was filled with army bunks and wounded men in blue pajamas. It was a world of difference from what I had been used to as a soldier in a mechanized company. There were actual beds to sleep in, there was running water available, and there was air conditioning. Such differences may not have affected every patient, but I must confess they did make a difference to me. I had slept so long on the ground that the hours spent in a bed were somewhat uncomfortable at first. The cool air coming from the air conditioner was a bit of a shock. I had spent all my time out in the Asian heat, and it took me some time to acclimate to refrigerated air. The same shivers must have hit quite a number of the combat wounded, because the medical types were ever ready with a blanket for those new patients who came in and lay shivering under the sheets.

I had often heard about army nurses, and I was looking forward to seeing a female or two. The sad fact was that I never laid eyes on a single female nurse the whole time I was in the hospital at Cu Chi. I don't know where they were, but they weren't with us. Maybe officers got female nurses. We got Lou Crosby!

Crosby was one of the nurses who ran the ward I was in. He was well over six feet tall, weighed about two hundred pounds, and had a no-nonsense attitude when it came to the boys in his care. For such a big bruiser, he looked over the bunch of us like a mother hen. Others came in and took their shifts as the ward nurse, but Lou Crosby stuck in my mind. He was from San Antonio, Texas, and that may have helped raise him to a more personal level of thought in my mind. Anything that smelled of home was welcome.

The doctors seemed to come and go as faceless entities that held the power of going home over the heads of those who had taken one for the team. I don't mean to sound disrespectful in any way. What I mean is that these men of medicine had so much on their plate that they could not waste a minute of their time with bedside manner. They were shorthanded and overburdened and simply came into the wards to take care of business and get on to the next case. The truth is that the only doctor's face I remember was the one who saved me from losing a kidney.

The consensus of medical opinions was that my right kidney had received such a blow that it would never recover and it needed to be taken out as soon as possible. This was what everyone told me, except for one army doctor with a Spanish-sounding name and an accent to match. My memory is a bit fuzzy on this, but I think he was Peruvian and not a US citizen. This doctor decided I had a badly bruised kidney that would heal itself if we just left it alone long enough. As a rule, the army doesn't let GI types lounge around in a hospital bed long enough for this kind of treatment to become successful. I have no idea how he managed it, but under this man's care, I was allowed to do exactly that. I don't even remember his name, but because of his insistence that my body would heal if given enough time, I have two healthy kidneys more than forty years after the fact.

So I settled in as a long-term member of the 12th Evac Hospital. I began to enjoy air conditioning and a bed with clean sheets and actual meals that were delivered to my bedside. I played poker with the other patients and with Lou Crosby, and I wrote letters home, telling anyone who would listen that I was none the worse for wear. All the time I kept hoping someone would come in and slip me the good news that the powers that be had decided to send me back home as soon as

I could walk fairly straight again. When someone did slip in and bring me some news, it wasn't good and it didn't have anything to do with my going home.

Track Twenty-Eight

CUE: *Where Have All the Flowers Gone?*,
THE KINGSTON TRIO

I had been in the 12th Evac Hospital a number of days when members of C Company began to drop by to see how I was doing. Captain Meilstrup and a couple of the others from the command group showed up one morning. When I asked them what they were doing in Cu Chi, I got some answer about having to give a report. I didn't really pay much attention to it, but when members of the 2nd Platoon showed up later in the day, I realized they were not there to give any report. When I asked what was going on, there was a shuffling of feet and some looks back and forth, and then they told me.

C Company had taken a pretty bad pasting during the attack on May 12. It was short on combat-ready tracks and men as well. In its wisdom, the army had finally decided to give C Company the stand down that was so long overdue. I was not there for the festivities. I was an inmate of the air conditioning and clean sheets at the hospital in Cu Chi. This fact may have saved my life.

Stand down is usually a time of complete carefree rest and recreation for those who are charged with taking the battle to the enemy. There were infantry stand-down areas in each of the major base camps. Some of the stand-down areas even had above-ground swimming pools to give the line troops a little relief from the ever-present heat. Beer and soft drinks were readily available in trailers filled with ice to keep them cool, along with hot barbecue and hamburgers, which seemed to be cooking all the time. Movies were shown after dark, and sometimes there were even performances by traveling musical groups from the USO. The whole affair was conceived to be a short departure from the strain and constant exposure to danger that was the life of those who lived beyond the base-camp wire. What is intended is not always what happens.

Stand down finally came to the battle-weary troops of C Company, 1st of the 5th. It was a chance to let down and feel what life was like inside the wire, without ambush patrols or night guard, which broke up the hours of darkness and cut sleep into fragments of about three hours a night. It was a welcome time for the company, which had been out for such a long time. Stand-down areas are reserved to a company alone. No one else is admitted there. At least, that is the way it is supposed to be.

On the evening of May 16, 1970, the company was climbing up into a set of wooden bleachers to watch a show put on by a rock 'n' roll band from the USO. A

group of men from one of the rear-echelon units in Tay
Ninh entered the stand-down reserve and began to help
themselves to beer and barbecue that was set out for the
infantry troops. Captain Meilstrup walked over and
informed the intruders that they would have to leave.
When they refused, he gave them a choice of leaving
voluntarily, having the MPs take them away, or being
removed by an irritated combat company. The answer
they gave was profane and disrespectful, and it caused the
whole company to come out of the stands and bodily
throw the intruders off the stand-down area. I have often
wondered what kind of logic would cause men to pro-
voke an entire combat-hardened company to rage in
such a way.

The men of C Company climbed back up into the
bleachers to await the show, completely ignorant of the
fact that one of the ejected rear-echelon troopers had
gone back to his barracks, picked up an M-16 rifle, and
returned to the stand-down area. There he opened fire
on the unarmed men seated in those bleachers. The
attack was sudden and deliberate and resulted in the
death of Joe Raber and Gary White and the wounding
of ten others.

When I heard this, lying in a hospital bed in Cu Chi,
I was stunned. I still am to this very day. It was completely unthinkable that an American soldier, much less one
who lived safe behind the wire and had never seen a day
of combat, had done this. It was so completely irrational
that I had a hard time getting my mind to wrap around
it.

I think what hit me hardest was the fact that Raber
had been sent back to the rear area to be the mail clerk
for the company. He was out of the fighting. He was just

waiting for his time to go home, and he was shot in the head by a man who was angry because he had been ousted from beer and barbecue, where he did not belong in the first place.

I realize now how lucky I had been. I was knocked around a bit by an explosion and dusted off the day before the big attack on May 12, and I was lounging in a clean hospital bed on the evening of May 16, when Raber and White and ten others were shot by a rear-echelon idiot. I have often pondered my good fortune in missing these two incidents. There seems to be no reason to it. It was just a matter of the draw, as it has been in all wars. It was not my time.

One of the odd circumstances of modern warfare added to the bizarre scenario of this stand-down shooting. The company, which used every imaginable type of weapon on a daily basis, was completely unarmed. When an infantry company entered a base camp, it was to disarm and check all its weapons at the company arms room. The logic seems to have been that combat troops were a bit trigger-happy and might shoot up the place if they were left in possession of their weapons. The reverse was true for the troops who lived inside the wire and stacked C-ration cases for a living. These garrison troops each had a weapon, which they kept in their barracks and could get to any time they desired. This piece of awkward thinking set up the shooting on May 16. Not even the maddest of rear-echelon troopers would have shot into a fully armed and battle-hardened combat company, for fear of what would come back his way. It was this odd circumstance that led to the murder of two and the wounding of ten unarmed and helpless infantry soldiers.

The shooter was convicted and sent to prison—but he served only six years. He walks the streets a free man today. We all know his name and where he lives, yet no hand has been raised against him. If I were that man, I would sleep in terror every night, knowing that there are still over a hundred men out there, somewhere, who have killed men for a living and feel that there is still justice to be had.

Track Twenty-nine

CUE: *Get Back*, THE BEATLES

Hospital stays in war zones seem to all be pretty much the same. Mine, I am certain, was no exception. The medical types seemed to have an atypical military attitude. That is to say, they seemed caring and interested in the emotional as well as physical welfare of their patients, and for the most part were amazingly easy to communicate with. At least that was how it seemed to me, so long as I was in the 12th Evac Hospital in Cu Chi. When my kidney began to function again and it was pretty obvious I was going to get well, I was handed the news that I was not going to be sent home. I was to be transferred to a rehabilitation center in Cam Ranh Bay. This was not the news I had expected, and I said so. In fact, I made a bit of a protest, which suddenly brought the military nature of my world back into sharp focus. I was put into a uniform and shuffled onto a C-130 aircraft and flown away to the north with very little ceremony. I found myself flung, head first, back into the army, which knew me only by number and rank. It was a bit of a shock after having spent such a long time in a small combat unit where I had a name and had become an accepted member of the family. I was once again just a cog in the wheel, with one exception. I was a cog that had combat experience, which made me a commodity that was in demand at that time.

The rehabilitation center was set on the beach right next to the naval base at Cam Ranh Bay. That beach was one of the most beautiful I had ever seen. The sands were soft and white, and the water was a deep blue. At the time, the rumor was that the Hilton Hotel chain had already purchased the area. It was assumed to be planning to set up a tropical resort there, as soon as the inconvenient war business was cleared up. That plan, of course, went south with the fall of Saigon.

I was logged in as a patient and assigned a bunk and a number of exercise classes to attend. Then I found myself in a formation of other recovering cripples, where a familiar question was asked.

"Who in this group is an Eleven Bravo?"

A number of hands were reluctantly raised. The sergeant in charge looked at us with cool eyes and had us fall out. We were ushered to an arms room and issued weapons, then paired up to be the tower and bunker guards for the facility. Here, once again, I felt the isolation from the rest of the army that becomes the familiar ground of the infantry. As we were loaded onto a deuce-and-a-half truck to be taken out to our new guard posts, I remember noticing GIs lying on the beach and swimming in the crystal clear water. I would get my chance to do that, but at the moment I was bathed in resentment for every man in the army who did not wear crossed rifles on his collar. I am ashamed to admit that resentment remains to a certain extent. It is a foolish and completely ignorant emotion, and I take no pride in it. It remains all the same.

The days at the rehabilitation center fade together in my memory. There were all kinds of exercise classes and volleyball games and stretching, along with appointments with the medical staff to check on our progress. Nights were generally filled with bunker guard, which was time spent looking out over the waterfront. There was no real enemy activity around that area, so we simply guarded the waterfront. It seemed pretty silly to me. I had to wonder if anyone had ever stolen a waterfront.

I suppose I had never turned loose of the notion that the medical types would notice that I was still stiff as a board and unable to run or jump and send me home, but no such message came my way. In fact, the opposite announcement was soon to come, with a bit of a twist.

I was sent over to the naval base to get x-rayed just one more time. The doctor in charge was a bit different from those I had dealt with at the evac hospital in Cu Chi. I think it is safe to say that he probably had never been in a position to see wounded coming in from the field, red with blood and still smelling of the conflict. I doubt he had been in a position to discover the depth of his patients' wounds with the sound of the dustoff choppers just outside. I suspect he was a bit removed from all that, therefore his attitude was stiff and distant, and even a bit haughty. He stared at my x-rays for a moment and then scribbled something on a pad. As I remember, he never looked up at me. He simply said, "I've sent three of you boys back home already today. I think I'm going to send you back to duty." He handed me the note he had just written, and I was ushered out of his presence. I assumed that was the end of it, but I was wrong. It got worse.

As I said earlier, a bit of value was placed on the heads of those who were experienced combat soldiers. I didn't know it at the time, but when a line troop was released as ready for duty, there was a bit of a scramble as to who would get him. Cam Ranh Bay was far north of Cu Chi and the 25th Infantry Division. The rehabilitation center had no obligation or responsibility to send ex-patients back where they had come from. This was pretty unwelcome news to me. Along with my release papers, I was handed orders assigning me to a unit of the 101st Airborne Division, way up in the I Corps area. This was just too much! If I had to go back to the war, I wanted to be with people I knew and trusted.

I gathered my meager belongings and walked out of the rehabilitation area. There was a fairly busy chopper pad across a barbed-wire fence, just to the north of the hospital. I had spent weeks watching the helicopters come and go from there. Now I saw it as my chance at a ride home.

I crawled over the wire and began asking if anyone was going to Tay Ninh or Cu Chi. No one was headed that far south, but I did find a dustoff chopper that was going a little bit south to a fire-support base, so I hitched a ride. It was the beginning of a three-day odyssey that had me hitching rides back and forth across the narrow country of South Vietnam, in all sorts of flying machines. No one ever questioned my motives or my right to climb onboard any aircraft that had room to take me. The secret seemed to be that so long as I was headed toward an infantry company or a combat area, I was welcome to go. So it went, until I finally reached the base camp of Tay Ninh and the rear area of Charlie Company, 1st of the 5th.

When I got to the company orderly room, I found 1st Sergeant Strain was in residence there. This was unusual, for during my time in the field, he had never spent much time back in the rear areas. Everyone there was surprised to see me. They were under the impression I had been sent back to the States. At first I was a bit confused that they would have lost track of me like that, then it hit me how many had been wounded and killed during the big attack in Cambodia. Not knowing what happened to so many was not strange at all.

Strain asked me what kind of shape I was in and looked me over with the trained eye of an experienced first sergeant. He made me bend over and try to touch my toes, and poked around on me a bit. It was obvious he was not pleased with what he found.

The company was split into two units, doing duty here and there until they could replace the tracks lost in Cambodia and get enough replacements to make a full compliment. Captain Meilstrup was due to be rotated out in a couple of days, and everything was up in the air, so I was assigned to man the radio in the rear for a few days, until Sergeant Strain decided what to do with me.

I settled into my position in the rear echelon fairly quickly. There were a number of men there whom I knew from the field. Lurch was acting as the noncommissioned officer in charge, and Larry Grubbs, who had taken my place in sniper's school, was now acting as the company arms man, or gunsmith. I moved into a bunk in the arms room with Grubbs and felt that this might be OK for the rest of my time in Vietnam.

Life in a base camp was so different from life beyond the wire that it took a little getting used to. I had been in a couple of hospitals for some time, so it was a little easier for me, but it still was a far cry from life with the company. My days and nights were split up. Some days I took radio watch during the day and relayed normal radio traffic to and from the company. Some nights were mine to sit on the radio and monitor what may be happening in the field and help with supply and dustoff calls when battalion could not do so. It was somewhat hard to sit and hear men I knew speaking in strained voices that came to me through the scratchy speakers of the radio. I listened as they dealt with deadly moments out there in the dark, knowing that there was nothing I could do but listen.

The base camps were huge and filled with all the support facilities of a whole infantry division. They also had entertainment and creature comforts for those who lived and worked inside the wire. The comforts were stark at best, but they were comforts none the less. One night, when I was not assigned to duty in the radio bunker, I went with Grubbs and Lurch to a club for a beer and a movie. The club was only a tin building with a bar and a few tables, but the movie and the beer were real enough. While we were sitting there watching Boris Karloff in a really bad horror flick, we began to hear the dull reports of rockets hitting the ground. Sirens began to wail, and we could hear choppers winding up and taking off, trying to clear the ground in an attempt to escape the attack. I looked around and discovered that the room was filled with rear-echelon types who were sitting and staring at the movie screen, giving little notice to the approaching sounds of explosions as the rockets began to hit closer and closer. I was squirming in my seat before some of the men rose from their tables and started leisurely walking toward the door, in the direction of the nearest underground shelter. The explosions grew louder and closer, but no one seemed to be hurrying at all. Then a huge explosion seemed to go off just outside, and everyone in the room fell to the floor, piling on top of each other in a heap. The knot of sweaty, green-clad men lay on top of each other on the floor until the explosions seemed to pass and get farther and farther away in turn. Then, without a word being said by anybody, the whole bunch rose and returned to their tables. The whir of the projector still running and the awful dialog from the movie were the only sounds that could be heard. No one left until the movie was over. When we did exit the tin building, it was impossible not to notice a huge hole in the ground, just outside, that was almost as big as the building itself.

On that night I gained a new insight into the life of those who lived inside the wire. Unlike the tracks, which moved and changed positions each night, the base camps were huge, stationary targets for the Viet Cong. Tay Ninh base camp was often called Rocket City because of the frequency of just such attacks as I experienced that night. Consequently, the rear-echelon troops who were stationed there were forced to live with the specter of huge rockets coming down on their heads as an everyday possibility. At least when we were out in the bush, the enemy had to look for us. The rear-echelon types just had to take it and go on with business as usual.

Just as I was about to settle in to this base-camp duty, Sergeant Strain demanded I present myself in the orderly room. When I got there, his face was very red, and he had some official-looking papers in his hand. He clapped his grey eyes on me and asked if I had any idea how many people were looking for me. The jig, of course, was up. My taking my leave from the rehabilitation center and ignoring the fact that I was officially assigned to some infantry company in the 101st Airborne Division had come to light. My reasons for returning to the 1st of the 5th seemed of little interest to the first sergeant, who was faced with a ticklish problem because of my antics. He explained to me in an irritated voice that he would have to give me up if the case were pressed, but that the 101st would probably not press the case if I were in the field on combat assignment. The problem seemed to be that I was still gimping around quite a bit and, despite the fact that the army had declared me fit, was in no shape to go into a combat situation. To send me out to that would risk my life and possibly that of someone who might have to depend upon me. Such being the case, there was only one other possibility of redemption.

Not far from Tay Ninh base camp was the legendary Nui Ba Den, or Black Virgin Mountain. On top of this three-thousand-foot extinct volcano sat the Nui Ba Den radio relay station. Combat companies of the 25th Division were charged with sending personnel to man the defensive bunkers on the perimeter of this tiny base camp in the clouds. As chance would have it, Sergeant Strain was due to transfer two men up to the top of the mountain as bunker guards. The usual practice was to send the cripples and the idiots up there to sit out their time in the war so they didn't hurt anybody else.

According to the first sergeant, my physical condition and my stunt of ignoring my orders and returning to C Company without permission qualified me as both. So with a slap on my back and the assurance that Sergeant Strain would also be up there very soon, I was assigned to sit out my remaining wartime high in the clouds, in a fortress that had already been overrun several times by the NVA. If that wasn't a spooky enough prospect, there was the ghost!

Track Thirty

CUE: *The Fool on the Hill*, THE BEATLES

The blades of the Huey helicopter bit into the air with that characteristic slapping sound. The sky all about us suddenly vanished into a swirling mist that obscured all vision and enveloped us with a touch like damp fingers. The cold caress seemed to fill me with a sense of dread and then vanished as we broke free of the cloud bank and made a wide turn around the summit of the legendary mountain. As we settled down on the flat surface of the landing pad, I could see that the place was pretty much like any other fire-support base or forward area encampment. There was one striking difference: it was pretty much all vertical.

Nui Ba Den was a place of legend, not only from centuries of Southeast Asian history but in American GI folklore as well. I had looked up into the night skies many times during the darkness of the ambush patrols and been fascinated by the halo of lights that seemed to float as a new constellation in the inky heavens. The Americans held the top of this awe-inspiring peak as the 25th Division radio relay. That being the case, the whole place was pretty much made up of holes in the side of the rocks and sandbagged bunkers, which jutted out precariously over sharply declining stretches of barbed wire and defensive mines. It was all ringed in by huge banks of lights that would have been right at home over Yankee Stadium. With this intensive illumination, the top of the mountain was visible at night for miles in any direction. It was a visible pinnacle, both by day and night, that few would ever set foot on. On that sunny morning, just above the ring of clouds, I became one of the few.

I was accompanied that morning by Floyd Vester, another banged-up veteran of Charlie Company, who was sent to the mountain to sit out his time. As we climbed out of the Huey and looked about us, Floyd was taken by the steep grade of the footpath that led up to the orderly room. As a shirtless soldier walked past us, carrying a case of C rations, Floyd asked him where we were supposed to report. "Up there," was the curt reply, as the man continued past us and disappeared down a steep path around a huge rock. Somehow I knew that from that moment on, all directions would be something like that.

After struggling up the steep path to the orderly room, we were logged into the company and assigned to bunkers out on the perimeter. I was guided to bunker number eighteen by a tired-looking sergeant with really faded jungle fatigues and a penchant for punctuating each phrase he uttered with the word "See." The path was pretty darn steep, and I stumbled more than once on the way down. My guide, who had a slight limp, seemed not to notice the extreme angle of our descent. Later I would come to realize that the altitude from the bunker line to the orderly room spanned almost three hundred feet, but on that first day, it seemed farther than that.

The bunker was pretty stark but amazingly solid. The basic structure was fashioned from railroad ties set back into a hole against the mountainside. Everything was covered with layers of sandbags, which would probably soak up the impact and explosion of almost anything the enemy might throw at us. The whole affair was topped by a sandbagged observation post. From this point, the view of the rice fields and forests below was absolutely breathtaking. On that first morning, looking out across the Asian landscape from such a dizzying height, it seemed impossible that anyone could get tired of such a vista. That, of course, was simply not the case.

Evidently there was a bit of a problem getting enough replacements for the mountain stronghold. When I got to bunker eighteen, I discovered that there was only one other inmate there. His name was Wooten, and he was a redheaded farm boy from Ohio who possessed a respectable sense of duty and almost no sense of humor. He and I would be the only inhabitants of bunker eighteen for some time to come. Others would come and go, and some seemed to be gypsies who were never assigned to a specific bunker for reasons that were never made clear to me. Despite those who came and went, Wooten and I would be the only ones to call bunker eighteen home for most of my stay on the mountain.

I stored my meager belongings in a corner of the dark, bare bunker and climbed my way up to the observation tower, where Wooten was on guard. As I entered the tiny observation enclosure, Wooten looked up at me for only a moment and then returned his gaze to the wide vista that was the view to our front.

"You the new prisoner?" His voice had a lazy, country sound about it, which immediately put me at ease. "Keep an eye out for a minute, will you? I need to take a whiz."

Wooten suddenly stood up and exited the tower, through the tiny door that was barely wide enough for a single human. I was left alone to look out over what would be my post. From that high place, one could see for miles and miles, until the land seemed to fade out into the mists of pure distance. The tower was placed atop the bunker, and the sides and top were also heavily sandbagged. The opening of this small enclosure was about four feet wide and covered with a heavy wire mesh. I knew that this was placed there to keep hand grenades from being thrown inside. It was a fact that made me realize that someone, at sometime, had experienced such troubles. The legendary stories of Nui Ba Den being overrun three times came to mind and put a bit of a damper on the majestic view that stretched before me.

The tower seemed pretty well equipped. There was an M-60 machine gun and an M-79 grenade launcher and of course, I had an M-16 rifle. The weapons were formidable, but what was really impressive was the cache of ammunition. Just behind the bunker was a miniammo dump that held cases and cases of all sorts of ordnance for the weapons we had in place. It was obvious that the architects of the mountaintop relay station had envisioned the possibility of a long and protracted engagement with the enemy in which there would be little chance for resupply. In such an action, we would be pretty much on our own. These thoughts ran through my mind as I took my first looks from the tower of bunker eighteen. I placed my slightly nervous faith in the words of Sergeant Strain, who had promised me that this would be like a vacation from the war. As it turned out, he was absolutely right.

The days settled down to a routine that was calm and completely boring. The nights were spent in rotating guard shifts in the tower, looking down at the steep slope of the mountain under the harsh glare of those huge lights. The object was to notice if anything human was poking around down there or might be coming up in our direction. The days were spent in alternating guard duty with the neighboring bunkers. Every other bunker had day duty every other day. That left time on alternating days for repairs on the bunker, maintenance of weapons, and the usual work details that such a military installation requires. It was a vast change from life in the mechanized infantry, and it took a little getting used to. Most of all, it was hours, hours, and more hours of staring down at the world below.

Nighttime provided the best viewing, believe it or not. The darkness below was often broken by the stark eruption of battle. Explosions and bright flashes of artillery impacts were often punctuated by the bright stuttering of tracer bullets, straying in staggered neon lines across the black landscape. Such sights became a hypnotic reminder that the war still existed far below us. The war was still very much a reality, and somewhere, out there in the dark, men I had served with were still engaged in just such deadly and terrifying moments.

It took no time at all for me to realize how tremendously fortunate I was. With this realization, an odd sense of guilt seemed to settle on me. I am told this is typical of combat soldiers who are plucked from the line for any variety of reasons. It may be a common syndrome, but it has stuck with me, in one form or another, since that time. It is not unlike the shadow that hovers near the title graphics in the credits of a motion picture. You don't really notice it all that much, but it is there nonetheless. Many do not feel this until they return home from such experiences as war. I began to feel it high atop Nui Ba Den.

The days dragged by with a monotony broken only by the weather. There were times when the clouds would envelop us completely and leave us with no visibility. The mists that surrounded the bunker were so thick you could see only a few feet in front of the wire mesh. If ever there would be a time for the NVA to press an attack on the mountain stronghold, the days we lived in the mists of heaven would have been ideal. We could get no help from helicopter gunships or jet fighters during such times. The clouds rendered us invisible to the world of aviation, and that meant resupply or reinforcements were out of the question as well.

When the clouds chose to keep us company for extended periods of time, the entire mountain command went on an energy-saving schedule. Because the electric power was provided by gasoline generators, and because gasoline must be brought up by helicopter, it was standard procedure to begin rationing energy to the bunkers as soon as it was evident we would be socked in for some time. What this meant was that every other bunker was to get electricity every other day.

The first night I was to experience this phenomenon of stewardship, Wooten and one of the gypsies picked up their weapons and a blanket and left the inside of the bunker before the lights were scheduled to go out. I thought this would be a marvelous opportunity to get some uninterrupted sleep. The interior of the bunker was constantly lit by a bare, 75-watt bulb that burned day and night. It shone in my eyes when I tried to sleep and caused my interrupted nights to be wakeful. I thought a quiet night of darkness would be a welcome thing. I couldn't understand why the others had chosen to go up to the tower. While I was wondering, the lights suddenly went out and the reason became obvious.

A slight rustling sound alerted me that something seemed to be moving in the darkness. The rustling grew into a scurrying and the scurrying into a forceful scampering, and I reached for the flashlight that hung by the door. The stark beam of the army flashlight revealed to me that the rough surface of the wooden floor had been replaced by a writhing, teeming sea of rats.

The sight caused me to grab for my weapon and a blanket and bolt up the stairs to join the others. When I got out into the dank, foggy night air, no one said a word to me. They just smiled and acted as if nothing had happened. I suspect they had been through the same experience when they were new to the mountain and its ways.

I came to understand that the rats were our neighbors in the bunkers. The massive layers of sandbags had created a sort of haven for the creatures, and they lived there almost unmolested, except by a few of our more ingenious attempts to keep them at bay. We built inventive rat traps and took target practice on them, but nothing really seemed to discourage the beasts. I have often wondered if the steady diet of GI leavings created a particularly hardy strain of rat or weakened them for generations to come.

Possibly the most intriguing element of the Nui Ba Den mystique was the infamous ghost. The stories are many in their form and probably all balderdash, but the mountain was a historic haunted place. It seems a Cambodian princess was killed by a tiger on its heights, and her spirit has been seen wandering around up there for centuries. The local population all believed in this legend and supposedly gave the summit of the mountain a wide birth. Whether that is true or not, the Americans can report, with some authority, that the NVA soldiers did not seem inhibited by the ghost stories. They ran all over the slopes of the mountain with blatant disregard for anything that didn't go boom. There was gossip among the American troops who were stationed up there that there had been incidents involving the ghost that were hushed up to prevent a morale problem. I never saw anything more frightening than the first sergeant in his underwear.

Speaking of 1st Sergeant Strain, he appeared to become the top kick of the Nui Ba Den Provisional Company a few months after my arrival there. One day, the field telephone buzzed in bunker eighteen, and I was ordered to climb the steep path that led to the orderly room. When I got there, Sergeant Strain handed me a packet of typed orders and placed his hand on my shoulder in a way he had never done before. "You made it," was his only comment. He turned on his heel and left me standing in the orderly room, where the clerk had me sign out of the company and told me I could go home on the next flying machine that landed up there. The words were barely out of his mouth when we both heard the signature throbbing of a Huey helicopter descending onto the landing pad.

The clerk shook my hand and I ran, stumbling, down the path to the bunker, where I grabbed my few belongings and climbed back up to the chopper pad as fast as I could. I crawled aboard the idling helicopter and felt the rotors pick up, separating the chopper and me from my last duty assignment in the Republic of South Vietnam. The pilot flew completely around the mountain to give me a last look and then dropped the nose toward the earth below. It was the last helicopter ride I would ever take and the beginning of the odyssey to get back home. Ever since that day, I have harbored some sympathetic understanding of the troubles of Odysseus during his long-suffering return to Ithaca.

Track Thirty-One

CUE: *Up on Cripple Creek*, THE BAND

The helicopter settled to earth on the landing pad, and the heat from the Asian soil once more seemed to envelop me. My time on the mountain had been relatively cool by comparison, and my return to the earth below was a heavy reminder of the withering heat that was very much the signature of that land.

I had been set down in the tiny fire-support base that was all that was left of what had been the huge 1st Division base camp of Dau Tieng. When the 1st Division was rotated back to the States, Dau Tieng had been handed over to the Army of the Republic of Vietnam. The only portion of a whole division base camp that was to remain American was a tiny corner that would house resupply and repair for the mechanized companies that worked nearby and a small artillery contingent. In their

typically ruthless mercantile fervor, the ARVN commanders had removed and sold everything they could lay
their hands on. This left the small group of Americans
surrounded by the skeletal remains of what was once a
formidable military establishment. It was pretty scary.
From the summit of the mountain, I had watched this
tiny camp take enemy mortar fire, night after night, and
I had no desire to spend any time there if I could avoid
it.

I was directed to the headquarters building, which was
the typical tin shed. Once inside, I came face to face with
the army that I had forgotten entirely. I was once again a
number and an inconvenience to the clerk who shuffled
papers for a living. I was asked to sign all kinds of forms
and then instructed to hand in a number of items, which
the clerk in turn had to sign for. I turned in an M-16
rifle, my helmet, and the rest of my gear, and then was
asked for a flak jacket. I explained that I had never had a
flak jacket. The supply clerk, who was eating a Hershey
bar, explained to me that I had to have been issued a flak
jacket. I explained to him that had to or not, I was never
given a flak jacket and did not have one to turn in. The
discussion turned heated at this point. The Hershey-eat-
ing clerk insisted I would have to turn in a flak jacket or
he could not sign my release papers and I would not be
going anywhere. My retort is not printable here, but it
did prompt the clerk to give me an alternative. He said
he could sign off on my release if my last commanding
officer signed off on the form indicating I had not been
issued a flak jacket in the first place.

I was stunned. What this rear-echelon creep was sug-
gesting was that I wait around until a chopper could take
me back to the top of Nui Ba Den and I could get the

commanding officer to sign on the dotted line about a flak jacket I had never even seen. Then I would have to wait around until another wayward bird dropped in out of the clouds and had room enough to fly me back down to Dau Tieng. The possibility of getting fogged in for days was very real, not to mention the fact that the NVA attack that had never materialized while I was assigned to the mountain might just take place while I was chasing the paper trail of the missing flak jacket.

I left the supply office and went across the dirt street to sit under the shade of a tin awning and drink a cold soda, hoping that a miracle, or at least inspiration, would come my way. While I was sitting there, I saw the same supply clerk who had given me such military grief leave the tin building and walk off down the street. I squinted hard at the building, and inspiration did, indeed, come to me. I sat there another fifteen minutes, watching to see if the clerk returned. When there was no sign of him, I walked to the bartender of the outdoor soda stand and borrowed his pen. I located the box on the printed form that indicated I had turned in a flak jacket to the supply clerk on the mountain, and I marked it boldly. I finished my soda and walked calmly back across the road and into the tin building, where I was processed out by a pasty-faced clerk who had never seen me before. I was given travel orders to the 25th Division base camp of Cu Chi. It was all so crooked, and yet so simple.

The stripping of the Dau Tieng base camp by the ARVN had caused more than a few problems for the American troops left there. One of the big ones was the fact that the airstrip was no longer inside the wire. Whenever a plane landed, troopers with machine guns mounted on jeeps made their way out to the asphalt strip and set up a perimeter to protect the planes while they were on the ground. Consequently, planes didn't linger long at Dau Tieng. That afternoon, three of us were hauled out in the back of a jeep to try to flag down a ride out of the place before dark came and the mortars began to fall. To say we were overanxious was an understatement. I began to notice that the penetrating calm that had been forced on me as a combat troop was beginning to give way. I was no longer acting like a soldier but rather like a scared American boy who wanted out of this place and to get back home. I suspect the untimely death of Joe Raber was on my mind. He had gotten so close to being out of the insanity when fate caught up to him. I did not want to run into a similar destiny this close to going home.

We heard motors and saw an Air Force Caribou plane circling and turning to land. All three of us stood up, gathered our belongings, and started walking toward the flight line, even before the small plane touched down. The sun was fading and we knew there would be no other flights after dark.

The plane slipped onto the runway and taxied to the place where the jeeps and we hitchhiking orphans stood. Two crewmen opened the door and threw out some red mailbags and some bundled packages. Then they started to close the door. We three hitchhikers ran up to the plane and yelled over the din of the motors, asking if they were going to Cu Chi. One airman shook his head and pointed north, indicating they were not headed south to the 25th Division base camp.

"Where you going?" the airman yelled over the roar of the spinning props.

"Home." My voice must have had a bit of ache in it, for the airman looked at all three of us and shook his head.

"Sorry," he said, and turned back into the aircraft, shutting the door behind him.

We stood there, watching silently, as the Caribou turned and taxied down the runway to get into position for takeoff. At the other end of the concrete strip the plane stopped and seemed to sit there for an unusually long time, then slowly it turned around and returned to the place we were standing. The back cargo door opened, and the airman stepped out waving to us. "Get in," he yelled over the roar of the propellers. From that day on, I have had a special place in my heart for the Air Force.

Once delivered to Cu Chi, I was checked out medically and financially, and my service record was amended to reflect all that I had been through. I discovered that I had a bit of a hearing loss, which would plague me in later years, and a few combat ribbons I wasn't even aware of. Then I discovered I was stuck in Cu Chi.

The employees of the airlines that flew troops into and out of Vietnam had taken that precise moment to go on strike, demanding some sort of increased compensation or other. The upshot of the situation was that no one was leaving Vietnam until this contract dispute was settled. I was informed that there were over five thousand men backed up and waiting at the 90th Replacement depot and Bien Hoa Air Base. Until they started to move, no one was going anywhere.

The replacement depot personnel were putting up tents and placing cots out on the runways to house the refugees. The army mindset being what it is, it was not going to let such a large group of men sit around doing nothing, so details and projects were created to keep the waiting troops busy. All of them were, of course, unpleasant. I would have been one of those tent-incarcerated inmates, but I ran into an old buddy who changed my luck and my residence.

Since I had no actual billet and no mess hall to eat in, I walked over to a building that bore a big sign designating it as the 25th Division snack bar. I figured there must be some form of food inside. There was, and there was also a surprise. Rick Morris—the soldier who had been in my infantry training platoon at Fort Ord and had been saved from combat duty by a quirk of fate a year before—was running this joint.

As it turned out, Rick was the quintessential lucky soldier. It was completely true that his talents would have been wasted in the infantry. He had found his true calling since I had last seen him. He was not only the boss of this overpriced hamburger joint but virtually king of all he surveyed. He served hamburgers and Kool-Aid to every soldier in sight while also managing a burgeoning business in local labor, provided by a bevy of Vietnamese women who were hired by the army to provide laundry and housekeeping services for the rear-echelon types.

Rick was aware of my situation and took pity on me. He saved me from having to be the man in charge of some garbage detail by making me one of the security guards at the fenced compound where the Vietnamese women were housed. I spent my days watching the gate to see that only those with work passes got in or out. I spent my nights visiting this enlisted men's club or that around the area of Cu Chi. I would return late at night to Rick's quarters and sleep in a bed with sheets, under the artificial breeze of a huge electric fan. One night I started to go out for a beer but was dissuaded by an unusually attractive young Vietnamese woman who was in charge of the ladies in the compound and I suspect was Rick's romantic interest. She kept me in the compound by plying me with a really awful Asian beer and asking me questions about life back in Texas. I finally became sleepy and gave up the thought of going out. Late that night there were several explosions in various spots around the base camp. I will never know whether the young woman knew of the sapper attacks and kept me out of harm's way or not. All I do know is that after the war, the army found huge tunnels under the base camp, some of which came up under the women's compounds like the one I had guarded. The tunnels of Cu Chi are now a part of the legend of the Vietnam War. I may have been closer to them than I knew.

I stayed in Cu Chi for five days, then was released to go on to the 90th Replacement Depot in Long Binh. The rain seemed to accompany me. Thousands of men were still stranded in Long Binh. The planes were not flying yet, and men were scattered everywhere, trying to keep out of the rain and to keep an ear open for word that their number was ready to board. In the midst of all this wet confusion, I ran into Chester Johnson, whom I had flown into Vietnam with and had promised that we would meet on the way home a year later. A year had passed, and there we were, both still alive and getting darned wet.

In the middle of the night I was awakened by a great deal of noise coming from all around me. I had been sleeping under a deuce-and-a-half truck, and when I crawled out into the rain, I discovered that groups were being called to begin the process of boarding aircraft that were headed out. The next few hours were a bit confused, but eventually I found myself sitting in a jet airliner awaiting takeoff. It did not seem real. The plane was air-conditioned, and the cool air seemed much colder after the dampness and the heat outside. A set of earphones were hanging in the seat pocket just in front of me. I picked them up and placed them in my ears to find a glorious orchestrated version of "The Yellow Rose Of Texas" playing as we taxied down the runway and rose into the air. For a Texas boy, it was thrilling.

The plane rose sharply and then leveled off and flew a straight course for a few minutes. Then the intercom clicked on and the voice of the captain came through those terribly metallic-sounding speakers.

"Gentlemen, we have just cleared the airspace of the Republic of South Vietnam."

The cheer that roared through the cabin was ear splitting. Oddly enough, I don't remember uttering a sound. My heart was beating too hard and fast. I looked about me and all I could see were the faces of very young men. Young faces that told varied stories. Some were hardened with the experience of combat. Some were tanned from the Asian sun. Some bore scars they would carry for a lifetime, but all glowed with elation to be going home.

The trip would take us to Japan, Wake Island, and Hawaii. After landing at Honolulu International Airport, our airplane developed a mechanical complaint that caused us all to be disembarked and herded into a baggage-check area inside the huge airport. There we were locked up like puppies in a pet store window. Since we were still refugees from a combat zone, and since we had not been cleared through US customs, we were kept away from the native population and the chance that one of us might just walk away, never to be seen again.

The baggage-claim area was a large room with glass walls, which allowed us to look out onto the passing civilian world with a great deal of longing. As I remember it, people walked by trying not to notice our sun-tanned faces as we stared at them, wide-eyed, through the transparent barrier. Couples carrying bags and bedecked with flowers slipped by, along with nubile females wearing nothing but bikinis who obviously noticed the stir they were causing and giggled to each other as our eyes tracked them. We were in this odd purgatory for a little better than three hours, watching what seemed like heaven pass by only inches away yet unable to partake of it.

Just when we were all beginning to think of making a mass jailbreak, an Air Force officer came in and explained that our plane would not be continuing the trip. He then began directing us into three groups. I have no idea what happened to the other two, but the group I was placed in boarded a commercial flight headed for San Francisco. As we walked down the aisle of the passenger jet to be seated in the rear, we could see the looks in the eyes of the civilians. It was hard to get a grip on. Some of the people were smiling and obviously glad to see us. Some simply would not look in our direction. One lady, assigned to an aisle seat, looked at me with tears streaming down her face. When she became aware that I was looking back, she covered her face and began sobbing, quietly. To this day I have no idea what she was thinking.

I realize now that we were getting an intimate preview of what we would encounter when we returned home. As the plane rose into the night skies over the Pacific and headed us on the last leg of the journey, we sat in uneasy anticipation of what we would find in the world we had left behind. It would be a changed world from what we had lived in, before the days of blood and uncertainty. Then again, maybe it was we who had changed.

Track Thirty-Two

CUE: *The Day the Music Died*, DON MCLEAN

"It was the best of times, it was the worst of times. It was the age of wisdom, it was the age of foolishness."

Charles Dickens tried his best to liken all ages, one to another, in the opening of *A Tale of Two Cities.* I wonder if in eternal retrospect he had any idea how close to the mark he had come.

As our plane touched down on the extended runways in San Francisco, great elation rose from the back of the aircraft. It was a combination of relief and euphoria. I suspect it was a sensation my father and my grandfather experienced after their times in the war. Indeed, it has probably been the same for all returning American veterans, save those who served the South so faithfully during the Civil War. Those who wore the gray went back to find their homeland changed forever and strange new values in place. It took me decades to understand that those who came back from the unpleasantness in Southeast Asia did so amid a wave of change that was sweeping over the land of our birth. On that cold morning, as we crawled off that civilian airliner in San Francisco, I doubt if we had any sense at all of the growing new mind-set in America. Before we reached our homes, it would become all too clear.

We were ferried to the Oakland replacement center in an army-green bus, which somehow took a bit of the exhilaration out of the triumphant return. We were once again in a United States Army that demanded all sorts of protocol. Upon reaching the replacement center, we were unceremoniously stripped of our jungle fatigues and sent into a shower built to handle a hundred men at a time. As we bathed and marveled at the clean hot water, our clothing was sent to be burned. It was a sort of funeral rite for all we had become in the past year.

I have no idea how many hours we wandered through the jungle of forms and instructions in Oakland. I can only remember that eventually, I stood with a number of other uncomfortable-looking characters, clad in a dress-green uniform, bedecked with all sorts of ribbons and badges. The new bits of color on the green uniform would tell my story of service to those who knew the code.

The group of men was halted before a set of large wooden doors that barred the way to freedom. An army chaplain stood before the doors and held up his hand for silence. As the crowd quieted down, the older man looked over the group with a gaze that brought us all up short. We sensed something important was about to happen. He lowered his hand and spoke in a clear and amazingly compassionate voice: "Gentlemen, the president of the United States and the secretary of defense wish to thank you for your faithful service to your country."

He took a beat and let that statement fade away. Then his voice changed, and he was suddenly one of us, as the combat infantryman's badge on his uniform silently indicated:

"I know that many of you have had to do some pretty hard things in the past year. The very fact that you made it back to stand here today means that you did your job, did those things well. Now you're home. . . . Don't ever f——g do it again."

With that, the huge doors slid open and we stepped out into the sunshine. We were home, and we were free to go where we pleased. I believe that was the strangest feeling I have ever had in my life.

Outside I found Chester Johnson waiting for me. We shook hands, flagged a taxicab down, and headed for the airport. While waiting for our flight to Texas, it became obvious that we were somewhat invisible to many of the people around us. Folks who were the typical model of middle-class America seemed to turn their eyes away as we walked by. That is, many did so. Others seemed to fall into two groups. Those who were old enough to have lived through World War II greeted us with warmth and a certain parental-type pride. Young people who were of college or even high school age looked at us with smoldering eyes and projected an open disdain. Chester and I were both taken aback by the attitudes, and we found ourselves withdrawing and avoiding encounters with other passengers. It was safer to just exist until we got back to Texas and more familiar ground.

As it turned out, even Texas was not completely exempt from the new wave of hostility toward those who had fought in Southeast Asia. As I made my way to my father's office on the campus of what was then North Texas State University, I was stopped by a pretty young woman who wore a headband and bell-bottom jeans that looked as if they had been washed in battery acid. She ran her tiny fingers over the combat ribbons that brought color to the front of my green uniform. She looked into my eyes with an anger that was overwhelming and asked me, "How many babies did you kill to get those?"

I still had a short time to do in the army. Like so many, I was sent to a training command to live out my last days as a soldier and bring along the new inductees. As a combat survivor, I would be charged with preparing the new men for what lay ahead of them on the other side of the world. During this period of service, I never ran into any of those I had served with in C Company, 1st of the 5th. Indeed, it would be three decades before I would see any of them again.

We had all gone to Vietnam and to the company one at a time. We arrived alone, and we went home the same way, leaving in each of us a sense of the unfinished and the unfulfilled. We shared the unexplainable experience of war together and then were split apart and left to fend for ourselves, after learning to depend on each other so desperately.

Thirty years later, the survivors of the 2nd Platoon would gather once again in the tiny town of Holden, Missouri. The Internet provided the means of locating and contacting those who had been swallowed up by time and distance. We were no longer young men. A lifetime had worked its will upon us, and we met as aging veterans of what had become only a sad footnote in the history of this country. Clements's close-cropped beard was snow white, and French had a silver mustache that was nothing short of sporty. Bradley and Vunak had both gained weight, and I had lost all the hair on top of my head. Lester still looked very much the same, as did Gilreath and Lieutenant Clark, yet the years had understandably turned us all into different men than we had been. We were different, and yet, as we talked and laughed and cried, the years seemed to fall away, and for a short time the young men we had been seemed very much alive.

Oddly enough, this gathering was at the invitation of the family of Joe Raber, who were holding a family reunion in honor of Joe. It was fitting. It was a blessing. It gave Joe's family a chance to spend time with those who had been close to him in his last days and who had loved him in ways that might comfort them for such a tragic loss. This time was a blessing for us as well. The years had left us with an empty place in our makeup. It was a place reserved for those who had shared a terrible time together but had not had time to decompress after such a deep dive into the depths of man's inhumanity to man. Thirty years later, in a tiny farming town in Missouri, we came together again and for three days were a unit once more.

As we separated and returned to our lives, we took with us a renewed relationship that is still very much alive. We talk on the phone and e-mail often. We send Christmas cards and jokes to each other. When loss strikes us now, we close ranks and send our love and respect to families who always seem unaware that their loved one was once admired and held dear by a group that is now so diversified but was once a family, forged and made strong in the fire that few truly understand.

The war is a long time gone now. As Americans we have all moved on and even immersed ourselves in new military conflicts, which have impacted the country in much the same way as did Vietnam. Life has come almost full circle for me since summer '69. I have had a full and wonderful life with a kind and understanding wife and friends who surround us and fill our days with goodness. The times that seemed so confusing to the world have given way to other times and predicaments that have been faced by new generations in much the same fumbling ways. The nights of blood and terror in the Asian darkness seem long ago and so very far away to me now. And yet, on summer nights when the Texas breeze blows warm and the darkness seems to take on a life of its own, I still drag myself from sleep, hearing the scratchy, metallic sounds of the radio that call to me from out of the undying past.

"Five Four Whiskey, . . . Five Four Whiskey, . . . Niner Four Oscar."

ROBERT SWEATMON attended North Texas State University before entering the United States Army. After being discharged, he taught history for almost three decades. In the 1990s he entered the entertainment industry, playing roles on television shows such as *Walker, Texas Ranger* and *America's Most Wanted*. He is best known for his recurring role on the internationally famous children's show *Barney and Friends*. He lives with his wife in rural Wise County, Texas, where he writes screenplays and directs independent films.